# The Business of Capitalism

# THE BUSINESS OF CAPITALISM

A selection of
unconventional essays on economic
problems of the 1960's

## Harold Wincott

Published by
THE INSTITUTE OF ECONOMIC AFFAIRS

First published 1968
© The Financial Times (Mr Wincott's Articles) and
The Institute of Economic Affairs

Designed and printed by the Westerham Press

# Contents

# Preface

The Institute's researches and publications are normally the work of academic or other professional economists, but it has sometimes found economic insight in people whose speciality lies elsewhere. Mr Harold Wincott is an outstanding example of a journalist who combines a lucid prose style and homely wit with an intuitive grasp of the essence of economic principle and its application to business and public policy. But his long-established weekly articles in *The Financial Times* are seen mostly by business readers, and the Institute thought many of them of more lasting value and interest to teachers and students of economics – in non-capitalist as well as capitalist societies – as an informed commentary on British economic history in recent years. We have therefore persuaded him to permit the Institute to publish a selection of them in book form, with accompanying charts or tables, so that they are available to a wider range of readers and to libraries.

Mr Wincott's articles may be read for profit and pleasure independently of his approach to and preferences in policy. Apart from the succinct summary and unstuffy appraisal of some of the leading events, crises and trends, Mr Wincott's articles carry the consistent theme by which he has judged the efficacy or relevance of policy in both business and government through years in which fashion in economic thinking has changed, often with little care for empirical evidence and even less for principle. That Mr Wincott's approach is receiving a more general hearing after the disillusionment with policies he has questioned is an additional reason for republishing his writings.

We should like to thank Lord Robbins for his Foreword and Sir Gordon Newton, Editor of *The Financial Times*, for his ready permission to publish the articles. Thanks are also due to Mr Jossleyn Hennessy and Mr Denis Thomas for their editorial contributions.

The Institute normally dissociates itself and its Advisers from views expressed by authors of the work it publishes. Its reason for publication is that its authors are presenting material that will stimulate re-thinking by the teacher and student of economics, the economist in industry and government, the businessman, the public, the politician and the observer of the economic scene. Mr Wincott's book should serve as an informative text on recent and current affairs, an encouragement to reappraisal of fashionable thinking, and a reassertion of the underlying economic truths which distinguish his writings from the ephemeral commentary of our times.

January 1968                                   ARTHUR SELDON

# Foreword

It was a happy idea of the Institute of Economic Affairs to persuade Mr Harold Wincott to allow the issue of a selection of his weekly articles in *The Financial Times*. There is no working journalist who knows better how to pluck the day than Mr Wincott: the occasion of his utterances is almost always intensely contemporaneous. But none know better how to invest the discussion of the passing moment with the overtones of the permanent issues. For professional economists who are mindful that their preoccupation with abstractions should not lose sight of eventual application, I can think of few experiences more thought-provoking than perusal of these papers, which in their beginnings were pioneering enterprises in this form of public discussion.

Mr Wincott is one of the most distinguished of regular commentators on finance; and, as befits a one-time Editor of the *Investors Chronicle*, he has a special flair for the business of the stock markets. The reader of his papers will find himself inducted by quite painless methods into the heart of the more controversial discussions of such matters of recent years – the duties of directors, the desirability of full disclosure in published accounts, the pros and cons of allowing the issue of no-par shares, and so on . . .

But the main focus of these surveys is on wider horizons. The ups and downs of security prices are themselves the occasion for deeper reflections. The stock markets provide the starting point for examination of the movements of the economy as a whole. I know of few pieces of financial journalism more striking and more challenging to further analysis than Mr Wincott's comparisons of the changes during the last few decades in the real value of investments in this country and elsewhere.

It would be a mistake, however, to depict the scope of these papers as in any way restricted to even the wider implications of the business of saving and investment. Mr Wincott takes the whole field of economic policy for his province. The reader of these papers will find himself considering the whole range of important outstanding issues – the distribution of property, the nature of incentive, restrictive practices, taxation, employment policy, the balance of payments, the machinery of government. There is little that is alien to his lively eye and penetrating comment. Even the most casual inspection of these pages is almost certain to bring to light fresh significant facts or novel points of criticism.

If I were asked to name the salient quality of these papers, I think I should sum it up in two words, humanity and candour. Expository skill and technical competence one takes for granted in anything that Mr Wincott writes. But these are qualities which can be found elsewhere in a department of journalism, financial journalism, which in our own day and in our own country – pessimists please note – has attained outstanding excellence. But the special characteristics of Mr Wincott's approach are the width of his sympathies and the frankness of his argument. He discusses his problems in terms of their implications to the welfare of ordinary men and women and at each stage he discloses with attractive forthrightness the grounds for his judgements. He argues hard but he argues fairly.

This collection will be a reminder to his friends of many of the qualities they most value in intimate contact with Mr Wincott; and to readers who do not know him personally, they should serve as some justification for the admiration and affection in which he is held by those who do.

ROBBINS

# 1

# Business and Politics

# On cutting off your nose
# to spite your face

14 January 1964

According to the Neddy staff, the following is (one of) a list of items on which there was broad agreement (at last Wednesday's meeting): 'Wages could not be considered in isolation from other forms of income. It was necessary to consider all forms.'–*Financial Times* 9 January 1964.

THIS is going to be a very elementary article, taken at a slow pace, in deference to Neddy's injunction. On pages 4 and 5 of the latest National Income Blue Book appears a table, headed 'Personal Income and Expenditure', covering the pre-war year 1938 and every year from 1946 to 1962. The first half of that table sets out the various forms of incomes, before tax. The second half, with which we needn't concern ourselves here, shows how we disposed of those incomes.

In my chart, these incomes are expressed not as absolute amounts but as percentages of the total of gross personal incomes. Thus, in 1962, gross personal incomes amounted to £23,796 million; wages, at £9,500 million, were equal to 39.9 per cent of that total. In 1938, total incomes were £5,076 million and wages were £1,920 million, or 37.8 per cent. And so on.

Most of the other forms of income need no explanation. However, I may perhaps make some comment on some of them. It is a reasonable presumption, I think, that such items as forces' pay, employers' contributions for national insurance and health, national insurance benefits, family allowances, war pensions, and so on in the main go to wage-earners or equate with wages. In fine, if you take all forms of pay, direct and indirect, the table understates what wage-earners get if you just take the item 'Wages'.

Secondly, these figures are shown before tax. It is probable that if we had a similar table for net incomes, wages, both absolutely and relatively, would bulk even larger in the net total than they do in the gross. It is possible that the wage-earners' proportionate share of the

net total would have increased even more since 1938 than it has
on a gross basis. (You will notice how moderate I am being in my
claims.)

However, even taking the figures as they stand, the showing is sufficiently remarkable. Comparing 1962 with 1938, the proportion
accruing to wage-earners has gone up from 37.8 per cent to 39.9 per
cent. The proportion accruing to all employees has gone up from 59.6
to 71.8 per cent. The casualties have been the self-employed – down
from 12.7 per cent to 9.1 per cent – and rent, dividends and interest,
which latter item is more than halved at 10.9 per cent in 1962 compared with 22.3 per cent in 1938.

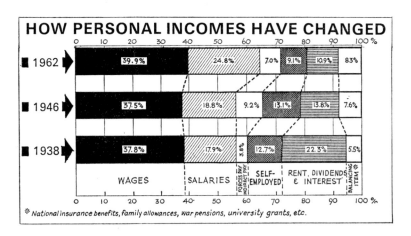

It is, of course, this item of rent, dividends and interest which is the
cause of all the trouble. So turn with me, if you will, to page 79 of the
Blue Book, where an explanatory note on this item appears. This tells
us that this item includes rent, dividends (including co-operative
society dividends) and interest *'received by persons and non-profit-
making bodies (including the life and industrial assurance funds of
insurance-companies and the funds of superannuation schemes)'*. The
italics, needless to say, are mine.

So we discover that this item 'Rent, dividends and interest received', which is the cause of all the trouble, has not only been more
than halved proportionately since 1938. We also discover that, despite
the heading of the table 'Personal Income', some of it is not personal

income as you and I understand it. Certainly it is not the sort of personal income which by the wildest stretch of imagination can be described as inflationary.

Are the pensions you and I – and many other wage-earners – hope to receive one of these fine days a source of inflation in 1964? Are the sums the life companies and the pension funds will pay to our widows when we leave this vale of sorrow a form of income Neddy must consider to-day? Surely, by providing for these things now we are preventing inflation, not causing it? Are we to believe the most astonishing heresy of all – that the dividend from the co-op is one of the reasons we're in trouble?

The true percentage of all rent, dividends and interest which finishes up in the hands of individuals – which is what irks some people – is, of course, wrapt in mystery. But since the total of this item today, including receipts by the life assurance companies and pension funds, represents as we have seen only 10.9 per cent of all personal incomes before tax, we might guess that gross rent, dividends and interest received by individuals is about 5 per cent.

Some support for this conclusion is provided by the annual statistics relating to interest and dividends on Stock Exchange securities published each year by the London Stock Exchange. The latest of these suggests 'that out of the gross total of interest and dividends for 1962 amounting to £1,959 million not more than £775 million can possibly reach the pool of personal disposable income. This would represent less than 4 per cent of the total disposable income for last year estimated at £20,000 million'.

Let's not argue too much. Let's say that 5 per cent gross – and the average tax rate on it must be pretty high – of all personal incomes from investment finishes up in the hands of individuals. Let's admit that this proportionate share is at most half what it was in 1938. Then will you pause to consider what an astonishing proposition is implicit in these figures.

Let's not be under any illusions. It seems that some at least of what we call the employers' representatives on Neddy have agreed that further punishment of capital and profits is necessary in an attempt to buy off labour. It seems that a Conservative Government under the leadership – in this field – of Mr Maudling is also willing to sell the pass. The great majority of the Press is equally convinced that some new form of taxation of profits will have to be produced.

## Business and Politics

It seems certain, therefore, that there will be an excess profits duty of some kind or another despite the fact that most of the evidence suggests that profits in Britain are too low, not too high. O.K. But let that decision be taken in the full knowledge of the facts. The facts are that the provocative item – in its broadest and highly misleading sense – is less than half what it was in 1938; and that we, the British people, are so eaten up with envy, hatred, malice and all uncharitableness that we shall proceed in the fulness of time to cut off the 5 per cent which represents our nose to spite the 95 per cent which represents our face.

Or is that second conclusion too harsh? Can it simply be that we as a nation are abysmally ignorant about the truth, which is what I believe I have set out in this article? Can it be that we have all been poisoned by the superb job of propaganda someone has done in post-war Britain?

That propaganda has not only long since succeeded in persuading us to accept a fundamental fallacy – that you can equate a residual (profits) with an inescapable overhead (wages) – which any butcher, baker or candlestick maker knows to be rubbish. It has succeeded in convincing everyone that profits are a form of income which, even if you take distributable profits, is less than half a truth. It has succeeded in convincing almost everyone that all property owners are Rachmans, all shareholders are functionless excrescences, and all rentiers are vampires sucking the blood of the honest workers and house buyers.

It has done this against fabulous odds. Against the odds of nearly 13 years of Tory Government; against a Press which is supposed to be predominantly on the side of free enterprise or capitalism or whatever you like to call it; in a time of methods of mass communication such as TV and radio the like of which the world has never seen before. I'd be very surprised if Dr Goebbels, wherever he is, isn't clapping his hands in admiration and confessing what an amateur he was. I hope you take comfort from that thought. You're going to need comfort from somewhere before you're very much older, you noseless ones.

# Should we be scared of the millionaires?

28 January 1964

FOR several weeks before my article 'On Cutting Off Your Nose to Spite Your Face', appeared here on January 14, a private correspondence had been going on between a reader of *The Financial Times* and one of our most distinguished economists (not Professor Wilson, although he comes into it as we shall see). I was privileged to sit in on that correspondence, on the understanding that I might discuss it in one of these articles.

The reader, who is 'someone in the City', was (and is) very bothered about capital values in the modern world of full employment and general prosperity. He quoted and, in a way, accepted the conclusion reached by Professor Thomas Wilson, Adam Smith Professor of Political Economy at Glasgow University, in his address before the British Association last September, that further redistribution of incomes had 'little to offer', since complete confiscation of rent, dividends and interest could only add 17 per cent to wages and salaries. And yet the reader rejected it because it 'completely ignores the fact that the wage and salary earner has little but his labour while the rentier and capitalist has his capital as well as his income.

Put into very approximate figures, wages and salaries have risen by about £1,000 million a year in recent years while the rentiers' and capitalists' share has risen by about £190 million a year – which fits in not so badly with Professor Wilson's figure. But the rentiers' and capitalists' increase in income has brought in its turn an increase in capital values of perhaps £1,000 million to £2,000 million a year [which] puts a very different complexion on spending ability or what might be called income potential'.

Given a 4 per cent growth rate and a continuation of even mild inflation, he went on, 'we shall have enormous capital figures in 10 or 20 years' time and millionaires will indeed be thick on the ground. Even if wage and salary earners are 50 or 100 per cent better off, it will be ludicrous to concentrate solely on incomes and equally ludicrous to state that "further redistribution has little to offer" '.

The economist in his replies made three points. First, a capital gains tax involves double taxation (of the capital as well as the income it produces); secondly, he questioned whether the non-capitalist in 1964 does lack the power of manoeuvre the capitalist

# Business and Politics

possesses (nowadays, with instalment buying, you don't have to be a capitalist to buy a house, or shares for that matter); and finally he emphasised that while 'national income' does not include capital gains in the sense of a write-up of the money value of existing assets, it does include all fresh capital assets created during the year in question.

On the final point, indeed, he quoted Neddy's proposal in its five-year plan that 25 per cent of all the additional output envisaged should consist of capital assets, compared with only 15 per cent in 1961. It's like the bees and the honey, the seed corn and the harvest. If we want the higher growth, we've got to have the assets.

In essence the City chap seems to be afraid of growth and prosperity because the rich will grow richer in a way that he will find socially intolerable. I'm quite sure that many other people in Britain share his fears. That, indeed, was obvious from the reaction of some of you to my article a fortnight ago. I must say I find it all rather depressing.

In this country – I've pointed it out before but it can't be said too often – on the evidence of *The Financial Times* industrial share index, there has been no appreciation in Ordinary share values in real terms over a period of nearly 30 years. The index is $3\frac{1}{4}$ times what it was in 1935; the cost of living index is $3\frac{1}{4}$ times. (Please, I'm not being Machiavellian in 'choosing' 1935, any more than I was in 'choosing' 1938 for my income comparisons two weeks ago. The base of the FT index happens to be 1935; the first calculations in the National Income Blue Book happen to be for 1938.)

It's not surprising on this performance that growth in Britain has been disappointing. In the United States, where growth has also been disappointing in recent years but which does have the highest standard of living in the world, the Dow average over the same period has risen almost $2\frac{3}{4}$ times in real terms. (The average is up 6.3 times; the cost of living $2\frac{1}{4}$ times.)

I would judge that millionaires are much thicker on the ground in the US to-day than they are here. I would also judge that there are many more American stenographers spending their holidays in Europe these days than there are British shorthand-typists holidaying in America.

For myself, I want to see Britain growing faster even if it does mean more millionaires, simply because I don't accept that it is any longer true to argue, as the old song did, that as the rich get richer the poor get poorer. I don't believe there are many millionaires who invest in

7

unit trusts, seeing that the average holding is £700. Yet the number of people using unit trusts, at 600,000, has doubled in five years, with a net investment last year of £60 million, twice as big as that of 1962, and altogether £371 million is involved.

I don't believe there are many millionaires (although I do know of one) who belong to investment clubs, yet the Wider Share Ownership Council last week reported that memberships of such clubs have grown in four years from 3,000 to 17,500.

I find it difficult to believe that all the readers of Saturday's issue of *The Financial Times* are millionaires. Yet the circulation of that issue has doubled in the last nine years. I doubt whether many millionaires are asking for a copy of the Wider Share Ownership Council's film, 'Take a Share', but the fact remains that the council is inundated these days with requests to show it.

We know from Mr Wilson's speech over the week-end that if the Labour Party wins the next election we shall have a full-blooded capital gains tax, which I suppose will please my friend in the City and all those of you who wrote saying how wrong I was in discussing the distribution of incomes to ignore 'tax free capital gains' (which, on a point of order, are neither income nor tax free).

We know that Mr Wilson favours a return to a two-tiered profits tax. This is interesting because I swear that the last Labour Government created the most glorious opportunities, with its company taxation and rent control policies, for the wide boys to become millionaires almost overnight in the share and property markets by takeover bids and quiet accumulation of sites financed by borrowed money. Oh yes, I know the thing only broke out under a Conservative government, but the seeds were sown by Labour and unless we're going permanently authoritarian, inflation has to break out some time. Come to think of the Russian rouble, it breaks out even under totalitarianism.

I wish we knew that the Conservative election manifesto would include proposals to extend to small savings made direct, and by individuals ready to paddle their own canoes, tax concessions similar to those made to people who do their savings through life assurance companies and pension funds.

I wish the Tories had the courage to admit that the short-term capital gains tax was a mistake in its present form and would be re-placed by a tax at a fixed rate. I wish they'd scrub the stamp duty altogether. I wish they'd take a long, cool look at the way what we call 'unearned income' is discriminated against by the Inland Revenue. I wish they'd adopt that idea of replacing crippling death duties with legacy duties (payable by the beneficiaries) which would help to spread personal wealth rather than wiping it out as the present system can do.

I believe such a manifesto would have great appeal, certainly to the floating vote and possibly to a wider audience. Come to think of it, have you noticed how Jim Callaghan has gone all quiet lately on his tax on wealth starting at £20,000?

Can it be that our Harold has told Jim to belt up? Can it be that our Harold – who whatever else he is, is not stupid – knows that every farmer these days must be worth at least £20,000 or damn near it; and that with houses costing what they do, and with National Savings Certificates, Premium Bonds, assurance policies, unit trusts holdings and so on thrown in, there are too many votes to be lost at £20,000? Significantly, our Harold said nothing about a wealth tax at Swansea. Where Labour draws back, we can be sure the Tories ought to strike.

# Nothing (much) to do with statistics

13 January 1965

A FRIEND of mine said to me recently that he didn't suppose Sir Alec Douglas-Home would know a season ticket if he saw one. (In the world in which I live you don't even have to describe it as a *railway* season ticket). I'm beginning to wonder whether this isn't an occupational hazard of the exalted.

Jim Callaghan quite recently said that Britain was making a greater effort than ever before to increase exports and productivity. Sir Robert Shone, Director-General of Neddy, has suggested we might be on the verge of a break-through in productivity.

This puzzles me. These chaps are terribly well informed. They've got their fingers on all the pulses. No out-of-date Bradshaws for them. All this I know. So I can only conclude they live in a world quite different from the world the rest of us inhabit. Let me explain what I mean.

It will involve me in part in speaking rather personally. You see, I moved a few months ago, and the move means I now use a section of British Rail which I never used before.

To be just, the old section gave me pretty good service. The new could hardly be worse. In the last few weeks, trains have been cancelled at the drop of a hat. They just tell you over the loud speaker, or pass it down the platform by word of mouth.

Once, at the London terminus, it's true, they did put up notices apologising to the customers and explaining why the trains were late. They had to take the notices down pretty damn' quick or there'd have been no trains at all. A break-through in productivity?

Because I moved, I had to send the car log book back to the licensing authority where I used to live, just to get the change of address registered. About a month ago I sent it, and not a word have I heard since. (I did write last week trying to buck them up because there's another year's duty due and I'm a law-abiding chap.) A break-through in productivity?

I don't know who's to blame here. It might be the local authority. Then again, it might be the Post Office. For there was the chap who wrote a letter to the Editor of *The Financial Times* a week or so ago, pointing out that letters postmarked 17 June, Walthamstow, E17, 9.45 am, and SE1, 9 June, reached him in N12 on 28 June. A break-through in productivity?

Lest you should say I'm always knocking the public sector, let me remind you of Mr Joseph Harsch's letter to *The Times* dated 29 June. Mr Harsch is a good friend of this country (a fact which has recently been acknowledged felicitously and officially), so he's pretty objective.

Last January, knowing he was going back to the States, Mr Harsch set out to buy his 'going home' Jaguar. This was no question of a British manufacturer fighting grimly for an export order in a hostile foreign market, swamped with attractive home products and other countries' exports. This was a customer whose only uncertainty was whether it should be the Mark II or the 'S' model, a customer who would collect and pay in dollars here.

Mr and Mrs Harsch are certainly triers. For four weeks they badgered one showroom, trying to get a demonstration, with no success whatsoever. They moved on to a main showroom, where they did get a demonstration, ordered the car and paid a deposit.

That was on 3 March, but getting on for four months later the car still hadn't arrived. Mr Harsch knew all about the strike at Jaguars, but his order was three months old before the strike began. A break-through in productivity? My next story has nothing to do with productivity as such. It concerns the son of a friend of mine who works in a highly unionised industry in the private sector. The son's working day starts at a quarter-to-eight. Officially, however, as he's 'broken into' an hour, he gets paid as from seven o'clock. He's supposed to leave at 5.15. Again, as he's 'broken into' an hour, he gets paid up to six o'clock. (In fact, he's very often home at 5.30 eating his tea, having taken half an hour to get there.)

Nothing to do with productivity as such, but an explanation why, to-day as in Mr Selwyn Lloyd's time, incomes are rising three times as fast as the output of goods and services on which they can be spent. Nothing to do with productivity as such, but an explanation of the widening gap between the weekly rates of pay everyone argues about and which mean little, and the actual earnings chaps take home and which mean a lot.

Well now, you may say there's nothing new in any of this. You may say there's not even anything new in the exalted ones claiming that we're all trying as we've never tried before to increase exports and productivity. After all, they've been saying the economy's never been stronger, or that we were rounding recovery corner, or entering a golden autumn, or were going to have a surplus of £300–£350 million on balance-of-payments account, year in year out, ever since I can remember.

With respect, there may be something new. Here, I'm just guessing, working on a hunch, putting two and two together. I start with the very strong belief that there's nothing the Americans want less than for sterling to be devalued. I add to that the knowledge that some of America's leading economic pundits are avowed expansionists, believers in planned prosperity, and so on.

I recall what the Prime Minister told his New York audience about the well-stocked shop which had all those thousands of millions of overseas investments, direct and portfolio. I recall that we are even now 'liquefying' the US investments our Government took over from us during the war.

I recall how the late Nye Bevan used to protest violently against the concept that men could be used as an 'economic thermostat'; how bitterly the Labour Party, in opposition, used to criticize the Tories when unemployment rose to a level which everyone in 1945 would have regarded as unbelievably modest.

My hunch? Simply that we are about to see an experiment – based on this belief that we really are on a verge of a great breakthrough in productivity – which will involve first the rejection of any serious cut-back in economic activity; and secondly the deliberate use of our overseas assets to bolster our reserves and protect the pound until the experiment succeeds.

Other people, I can only conclude, share my views; witness last week's figures from the Board of Trade showing that our industrialists anticipate substantial increases in capital spending this year; witness the Leyland Group's intention to spend £60 million on expansion over the next four years.

If we are right, will it come off? Mr Aubrey Jones, chairman of the Prices and Incomes Board, was saying over the weekend, I see, that the British worker was not interested in production, which is what I've been demonstrating in this article.

He further said that we needed two therapies, the first (the Government's job) to deal with the immediate fever, the second (which is presumably Mr Jones's job) long-term to ensure that the fever never happened again.

I myself have argued the case for raising a long-term loan, if necessary on the security of our overseas assets, to bolster our reserves while the British economy has a straight run at achieving a break-through. But I did stipulate that at the same time we should take every possible step to make the British economy competitive, the steps including a reduction in our tariffs, so that neither management nor labour could abuse their strengths.

Well, we've reached the position now where we impose substantial fines when management abuses its monopolistic strength, with the hint that next time someone may even go to prison for doing so. But so far as labour is concerned we're still in the we-are-the-masters-now-they-said-we-should-we-said-we-wouldn't-and-we-didn't stage.

For myself, I believe Mr Aubrey Jones' first fever places an impossible strain on human nature. I always thought that that saintly man, Sir Stafford Cripps, when he was conducting a somewhat similar experiment, made the basic mistake of assuming that our working population, all 25 million of it, was made up of little Crippses.

It isn't, any more than it's made up to-day of little Callaghans or little Shones.

So I conclude that, if my hunch about this Government's intentions is right – and we don't get the essential pre-condition I have insisted upon – this experiment will in the fullness of time finish the way the Crippsian one did. I hope, very sincerely, I'm proved to be wrong.

# The business that found itself

16 March 1965

THE heart of this article is getting on for six months old, which may suggest that the article itself is not all that topical. However, so far as I know, the matter has not received very much publicity. This seems to be a pity, for the issues involved could be of vital concern to all of us.

But let's stop being cryptic, and recall that a few weeks back the Bradford correspondent of *The Financial Times* recorded that on 23 February the 16-month-old dispute at the Baildon dyeworks of William Denby and Sons was officially declared by the union involved to be at an end.

William Denby isn't a big company; its assets are valued at just over £800,000. Its business is dyeing, finishing, proofing and shrinking of worsted and woollen cloths and gabardines. It also processes all types of synthetics.

It operates in what its chairman, Mr Philip Wright, himself has described as a contracting industry. Imports are a constant threat. The company lives on specialised trade and on the residue of business which textile businesses don't find it worthwhile to do themselves. But you can hardly describe a business (of this size) which in the last five years has financed over £400,000 of capital expenditure from its own resources as a backward concern.

So much, very briefly, for William Denby's background. Now for the strike at the company's Baildon dyeworks. This began in October, 1963, when some workers walked out in protest because a foreman had operated a machine in a mealbreak. It seems to have been a pretty old-fashioned sort of strike.

The company immediately sacked all 250 union members employed at Baildon – including, according to the FT man at Bradford, some who were off ill at the time – gradually replacing them with non-union workers. The strike was at times a violent affair, with fights between pickets and workers, vehicles stoned and damaged, and a worker who had been expelled from the union involved – the National Union of Dyers, Bleachers and Textile Workers – claiming that he had been punched in the face.

In the upshot, it cost the union almost £90,000 in benefits and so far as one can see 16 months of hardships achieved absolutely nothing for the workers. Last October, it was reported that a hundred of them had found other jobs, 40 had gone back to the firm, and the rest were still unemployed. The union organiser bought shares in the company and attended the annual meeting to plead unsuccessfully to shareholders to find a solution to the 'unpleasant position' where others had failed–the TUC, it seems, had rejected an appeal to help in settling the dispute.

The company side was put at considerable length by Mr Wright in the annual report for the year to 30 June last, issued in September. 'We are not,' he said, 'anti-union, we never refused to recognise their union, we never refused union representation, we pay 50 per cent above trade union negotiated minimum rates, but we were determined to exercise our right of selecting our own labour . . .

'The trouble makers were not coming back . . . (Mr Wright argued they had been responsible for many previous disruptions). A post-entry closed shop, whereby we could engage and select our own labour, provided it joined the union after engagement, would have surmounted all difficulties, but no, it was to be "status quo" or no union at Denby's, and so no union it was.'

So much, briefly, for the background to the strike. I can only describe it on the evidence available. I certainly wouldn't set myself up as adjudicator on it. My real purpose is to stress what I described in the first paragraph of this article as the heart of the matter.

This is contained in the figures set out in the panel which accompanies this article – figures which were provided by Mr Wright in his report. It so happened that the year fell naturally into three almost exactly equal periods. The first, of 79 working days, consisted of four months 'under union domination with double shift working'; the second, of 83 working days, was the four-month period 'on our own with a few loyal employees training new men'; and finally, there was the third period, also of 83 working days, 'with an adequately trained day shift'.

---

### FINANCIAL CASE-STUDY OF THE STRIKE

| Period | Production (in pieces processed) | Turnover | Profit after all charges but before tax | Proportion of year's profit |
|---|---|---|---|---|
| | | £ | £ | % |
| 1. July 1, 1963, to October 31, 1963 (79 working days) | 37,667 | 282,618 | 22,068 (7.81 % of turnover) | 20.93 |
| 2. November 1, 1963, to February 29, 1964 (83 working days) | 26,416 | 204,761 | 22,446 (10.96 % of turnover) | 21.31 |
| 3. March 1, 1964, to June 30, 1964 (83 working days) | 39,282 | 295,247 | 60,875 (20.62 % of turnover) | 57.76 |
| *Totals for Year* | 103,365 | 782,626 | 105,389 (13.47 % of turnover) | 100.00 |
| *Totals for Previous Year* | 131,446 | 923,715 | 61,509 (6.66 % of turnover) | |

---

The comparisons in the table are absolutely shattering. As Mr Wright said: 'Although our overall production has been 22 per cent less (than in the year to 30 June 1963), our pre-tax profits are 70 per cent higher, and the percentage profit on turnover has been more than doubled. In fact, we made almost as much profit in the last four months of the year as we made in the whole of the previous year.'

It was not surprising in the circumstances – the production in a single shift of more than five-sixths of what had been produced previously in two shifts, and with half the number of men – that Mr Wright waxed a bit lyrical. 'Our men now earn more than they have ever earned before. The flood gates of production have been opened. The restrictive practices have been swept away. The shop steward's eagle eye no longer spies to ensure that not one piece too many is produced or not even ten minutes' overtime is worked.'

You can be as cautious as you like in the conclusions you draw from

## The Business of Capitalism

these figures. Mr Wright himself said they were not published as a yardstick with which to measure William Denby's future. It can be dangerous to argue from the particular to the general. William Denby's experience before the strike at Baildon may not be typical of what goes on in British industry as a whole. The company's success in initiating what was presumably unskilled labour into the mysteries of a new craft in so short a period might be difficult to repeat elsewhere.

But knowing what we do know – or, more accurately, suspecting what we do suspect – about the widespread misuse of our manpower resources, about the manner in which restrictive practices encourage work-spreading and hold back productivity, about our poor showing in the international league tables, he would be a bold man who said William Denby *was* an isolated case, or that a great many other British undertakings could not achieve a similar increase in productivity and profitability.

If that happened, of course, this country's prospects would be revolutionised. There would be no more stop-go, no talk of devaluation, our balance of payments problem would be solved, we wouldn't have to bicker about overseas investment, we should have all the manpower we wanted to modernise our economic and social structure, the national revenue would soar, and so on. We would, in fine, stop being the sick man of Europe and take our rightful place among the industrial nations of the world.

One question remains in contemplating the possibility of that truly wonderful prospect. Do we, as a nation, have to go through the bitter experiences everyone associated with William Denby had to go through to learn the way to a new life?

I believe the William Denby episode confirms what many of us have suspected – that in this post-war era, we – we, the nation, not just managements – have too often been willing to attempt to buy industrial peace at a price which, long-term, has been much too high. I believe further that many of our responsible trade union leaders have felt that too often their position has been undermined by management's readiness to concede the demands of irresponsible elements among the workers.

Maybe we, as a country, can achieve what William Denby achieved without the stone-throwing, the punch-ups, the waste of resources, human and financial, Baildon saw. We must pray that this may be so.

If not, we shall have more Baildons before we achieve national solvency. Paradoxically enough, the better documented and publicised they are, the fewer we shall need.

# Capitalism—or a giant Co-op?

20 September 1966

I WAS suggesting last week, with the aid of various experts, that the London Stock Exchange hasn't been very successful in erecting the reliable signposts which are supposed to direct the nation's savings where they will do most good.

I'm not sure that I would go all the way with Mr A. C. Rayner who, in 'Higgledy Piggledy Growth Again', thought a pin would do the job as well as the back pages of the Pink 'Un. I don't know exactly what methods the Alliance Trust up in Dundee used in turning $2 million into $86 million in under twenty years without costing the British economy a single new dollar. But I'm darned certain they didn't include a pin.

For myself, I subscribe to the Thorman doctrine, which is that the Stock Exchange generally gets the main direction right, both ways, but spoils the effect by exaggeration, again both ways. 'Sound shares,' says Mr Thorman, 'are normally over-valued, and the shares which carry varying degrees of risk are normally undervalued.' Holders over recent years of Legal and General, on the one hand, and Imperial Tobacco, on the other, would hardly dissent.

But on the whole I think we must accept that the London Stock Exchange hasn't erected very reliable signposts over an extended period. This isn't a criticism of the Stock Exchange itself, which, except over the shortest period, fixes prices at its peril. Is it then a criticism of the British investment community, which does fix the prices?

*A priori*, the answer on the whole seems to be no, for as we have seen in their North American operations, given the right background and the right tools, our investors are no slouches at the game.

Mind you, I think that, as in so many other directions, British conservatism has played a part in this problem we are discussing. Our investors got Great Universal Stores wrong when it would have paid abundantly to get it right because they thought the company was expanding too fast, was relying too heavily on borrowed money, would run into heavy bad debts, and so on. Sir Isaac Wolfson woke up to the basic trends in the post-war British economy much earlier than most of us.

This apart, however, there are other fundamental factors which have militated against successful investment here over the period we are looking at. First, the British economy has been hit over the head with unfailing regularity and increasing severity every so often throughout the post-war period, which must have upset financial as well as physical investment programmes more than somewhat.

Secondly, as American experience has shown, much of the most successful investment in this modern age tends to be concentrated in the new industries. And you do have to be a wealthy country, it seems, to be able to afford successful new industries.

But above and beyond all this, what really bothers me is that on the whole so very few people in this country give a damn whether the investment community is properly served or not. I'm not referring now to the sordid scandals which have been an increasing feature of the British company world in recent years, which no one seems to be able to do anything effective about. Goodness knows, they're worrying enough, but they don't affect the great majority of British companies.

I'm not referring to the pillars of the company world who think so little of their shareholders that they fix up snug arrangements for making money for the selected few, with the aid of the shareholder's money, without so much as asking shareholders' permission, revealing though that attitude of mind is. Here again, praise be, only a tiny handful of companies is involved, and conversion, belatedly, is happening.

But in general, for as long as I can remember, it has been a tradition in the British company world to tell the investment community as little as possible as seldom as possible. It has been accepted that if you overstate profits and assets you may finish up in the Scrubs, but that it is highly respectable and jolly conservative to understate them. Is it any wonder then that the Stock Exchange exaggerates, erects the wrong signposts?

It would be unfair to mention names because this tendency has been so widespread. But it is a fact that a well-known business in 1947 told its shareholders, with a perfectly straight face, that the asset value of their shares was 63s 6d and that earnings were $45\frac{1}{2}$ per cent on the equity. In 1948, the asset value was seen to be over £13, and equity earnings 250 per cent.

It was the 1948 Companies Act, with its insistence on consolidation, which wrought that transformation. In the ensuing twenty years (this seems to be the normal gestatory period between Companies Acts in Britain) things got better. But it would be foolish to pretend that the investor has been properly served since 1948.

The spate of take-over bids which started in the early fifties brought some astonishing revelations about the real value of some companies' 'trade investments'. Such investments, which had appeared year after year in the balance sheet at purely nominal figures, were sometimes suddenly seen, when the investment was taken over, to be worth 10 times as much as shareholders had been led to believe.

Moreover, this major reform of consolidation in company accounts which the 1948 Act brought can, in the new world in which we live, result in consolidated company accounts now concealing more than they reveal. I have referred before this in these articles to the new generation of managers which has grown up believing passionately in diversification, that 'we can manage anything', and that where management teams have been built up they must never be broken up but must have new businesses bought for them to run.

I'm not concerned here to judge whether this process has been successful or not. Dr. F. R. Jervis, in his recent booklet* quotes a whole string of cases where it has been publicly admitted that diversification has brought serious losses, but we just don't have the evidence on which to judge the trend as a whole. All I'm saying is that unless and until all diversifying companies 'account by divisions', giving capital employed, sales and profits for each, the investment community and the Stock Exchange can hardly be expected to fulfil their proper economic functions.

I could go on for a long while in this vein, discussing, for example, the economic repercussions of non-voting shares where such shares have resulted in the assets of a company not being deployed to

*The Company, the Shareholder and Growth, Institute of Economic Affairs, 7s 6d.

maximum benefit and in the creation of self-perpetuating oligarchies; to the frequent lack of up-to-date valuations of fixed assets, which makes it impossible to calculate true return on capital employed; to the distortions in share values which can be caused by 'insider dealings', and so on, but there's a limit to my space.

I must also acknowledge that the Stock Exchange itself has done a great deal to put these and other matters right, and that its lead has brought a very good response from the majority of the companies the shares of which it quotes.

But it seems to me that we still lag far behind the US in this field (equally we are, with all our faults, well ahead of many other countries). In these conditions it is not at all surprising that Stock Exchange investment has been more intelligent and successful in the US than it has been in Britain over the last quarter of a century. It has too often been a sort of Blind Man's Buff, which may be good fun but is not calculated to make for an efficient and well run economy.

I would like very much to believe that the investment community will be given the chance to do a better job by 1990. It will not do so unless and until we make up our minds whether we want capitalism to continue, let alone to work efficiently, or whether we think we can run Britain as a species of giant co-op.

# Open letter to Sir Frank Kearton

1 November 1966

D EAR SIR FRANK – We have met, but I don't think we could claim to know each other personally. However, as a journalist, I have, of course, watched your progress and read your pronouncements with the greatest interest.

In particular, I read with fascination the summary of your speech to the American Chamber of Commerce last week in which you said, among other things, that in your old age you had come reluctantly to recognise that our present Government seems to have a better appreciation of business matters than its Conservative predecessors did.

Business and Politics

You'll get into a lot of trouble for saying such things, of course. I know. I, too, had to make a speech a week or two ago. I didn't say what you said about the present Government, because honestly I don't think it's true (of which more later). But I did say I thought Mr Wilson had shown a lot of courage on 20 July, and I did say that I didn't much mind which party put things right here, provided somebody did. Some of the chaps there – they *were* industrialists in the Midlands, which explains a lot these days – were absolutely livid with me.

But I'm not sure that when I talk of putting things right here, my ideas would agree with yours. For among the many things I mentioned to the chaps in the Midlands was the Labour Party's attitude towards profits. Now I know the Labour Party *says* it's in favour of profits. But I suspect it's only come round to favour profits provided they – the profits – do shareholders no good.

As Mr Anthony Wedgwood Benn, that bright young spark at the Ministry of Technology told Joe Rogaly of *The Financial Times* a few weeks back: 'We want the most successful possible British industry and profit is of course a criterion of success. *But the question of how you divide the profits, once made, is another subject.*' (My italics, needless to say).

Now this is where you come in. After all, before you rose to your present eminence in Courtaulds the profit record of the company wasn't all that good, was it? I'm a bit more sophisticated than the Minister of Technology. When I want to judge the success of a business I don't just look at its profits. I go for the return on capital employed.

And, frankly, the Courtaulds' record of earnings on capital employed was lousy – from 16.8 per cent in 1953–54 straight down to 7.8 per cent by 1958–59. Indeed, had we known in the latter year what we discovered a few years later, when Paul Chambers was breathing down the back of your neck, about the true value of the capital Courtaulds was employing, the picture would have been even worse.

Moreover, you not only know that profits and earnings on capital employed are important, you know it matters a helluva lot, despite what young Tony says, how they're divided; that they do do shareholders a bit of good. That unnecessary cut in the Courtaulds interim, just about a month before ICI made its famous pass at your company, very nearly put the lid on things, didn't it? And but for those splendid projections of profits and dividends in the future, a fate worse than death awaited you, didn't it?

All this must surely mean that you're the very chap to educate our present masters. But I must confess I'm a bit bothered by another speech you made. This one was in Cardiff early in 1964.

You were then arguing, you may remember, that industry should accept that its total profits as a percentage of national income should be restricted 'by and large to a given figure'. What that figure should be you thought to be a matter of political and social importance, and, you said, you were not very much worried whether it was the (then) current proportion or slightly higher or slightly lower.

Admittedly you were talking about total profits, but in the light of your earlier experience with ICI, I must say your remarks reminded me a bit of the old Rabelaisian tag. You remember? 'The devil was sick, the devil a monk would be; the devil was well, and the devil a monk he'd be'.

Not only that, but at the time I looked up the figures in the National Income Blue Book and I found that the proportion which total company profits bore to the national income had been declining pretty steadily from a peak of 21 per cent in 1951 to 15.5 per cent in 1962. (It has since recovered a bit, to 17 per cent). I thought that trend might have something to do with the fact that our gross fixed assets formation was a good deal lower than that achieved by most of our international competitors.

You went on to say something else that interested me a great deal. You said that you personally had no objection to an extension of the capital gains tax, which meant presumably bringing long-term capital gains into the net.

Why was I so interested? Well, you see, I'm even older than you are. So old that I can remember the famous occasion in 1928 when Courtaulds decided to issue what some of my journalistic colleagues delight in calling 'free shares' – an issue of one for one, it was.

I remember so well the headlines in the newspapers – 'Courtaulds Plum for Shareholders'. It proved to be a pretty sour plum. It cost £912 in good 1928 pounds to buy 100 Courtaulds just before that 'free issue'. Thirty years later, the holding, as increased by a further 'plum', was worth £670, in not nearly so good 1958 pounds. Just before the ICI bid the value of the holding was a little below £800.

## Business and Politics

Because of that bid, many brands were snatched from the burning, and to-day, despite your present troubles, I reckon the present market value of the original 1928 investment of £912 to be just over £2,000. But whereas the market value of the investment has little more than doubled, the cost of living has risen since 1928 at least three-and-a-half-times. Is it a capital gains tax you approve of, or a capital levy?

Interestingly enough, you said these things at Cardiff shortly after Mr Harold Wilson had made his famous speech at Swansea. Had you said at Cardiff in 1964 that you had no doubt Labour *would* be better for business than the Tories I could have understood it.

We were all pretty fed up with the Tories then, and not without reason. And Mr Wilson said some splendid things at Swansea. (They were so splendid I've cherished a copy of his speech ever since.)

Among other things, he said that Labour would be better at galvanising our sluggish, fitful economy than the Tories were. He said that Labour would not force on the nation a structure of high long-term interest rates with all that meant for investment. He said that Labour could ask for an incomes policy because it had 'clean hands, with no responsibility for the faith-breaking interference with collective bargaining and industrial conciliation and arbitration that were involved in Mr Selwyn Lloyd's pay pause'. He said that Labour was pledged to sustain growth. He said that one export which would fall sharply under a Labour Government would be the export of British scientists.

Well, we're men of the world – old men of the world, you might say – and we know what politicians' promises are. But I must say your present faith in Labour, after all that's happened in the last two years, does rather remind me of what Dr. Johnson had to say about something or other (second marriages I think it was) being a triumph of hope over experience. I must say you're in a pretty small minority among industrialists to-day.

But there we are. This is still, thank God, a free country (more or less) and you're entitled to your views. Anyway, we need men like you, if ever the Labour Party is to become in Britain what the Democratic Party is in the United States.

So keep on saying that Charles Wilson was right in pronouncing that what was good for General Motors was good for the United States. Indeed, if you prove that what is good for Courtaulds (not forgetting Courtaulds' shareholders) is good for Britain, we shall all be in your debt.

And stop worrying about what proportion total profits should bear to the national income. Your job is to see Courtaulds earns the biggest profits it can. To judge from yesterday's papers, that should keep you pretty busy.

# A job of work for Lord Campbell

8 November 1966

I'VE no idea of the order in which you read the leader page of *The Financial Times*. All I would suggest is that, to-day, if you intend to read this article (which, of course, may be a gross presumption on my part) you should first read the letter to the Editor from Lord Campbell of Eskan. This is what Lord Campbell's letter said:*

Lord Campbell, as you will know, used to be Sir Jock Campbell. His main job is to be chairman of Booker Brothers, which company has done magnificent work in Guyana. Like Sir Frank Kearton, Lord Campbell hasn't been afraid to announce publicly that he supports the Labour Government, which attitude has got him, too, into trouble, although I myself have always had the greatest respect for him, as indeed I have for Sir Frank.

*\*Harold Wincott, in his open letter (1 November) to Sir Frank Kearton, has – most entertainingly as always – added to the confusion and misunderstanding about the role of profits. And so he has contributed to the lack of confidence between businessmen and the Government – which is already bad enough in all faith.*

*Harold Wincott treats profits as though they were a sole end in themselves and seems to suggest in the last paragraph of his letter that Sir Frank Kearton's only object in life should be 'to see that Courtaulds earns the biggest profits it can'.*

*Businesses exist to produce wealth, manufacture and distribute goods, and provide services. And their Managers have to recognise and balance responsibilities to their fellow employees, and customers, and the community as well as to shareholders. But of course they must make proper profits: not only because of their clear responsibilities to shareholders, but because if they don't produce an adequate return on capital employed they will not be able to stay in business let alone expand and modernise. An inefficient, unprofitable business is a fraud on society. Certainly businessmen must aim to have satisfied shareholders – or they won't get financial backing for the business. But equally they must aim to have satisfied employees – without whom they cannot obtain skills and work; and satisfied customers – without whom there won't be any business. Moreover big businesses must come to terms with the society in which they are rooted.*

*I cannot understand how a man as intelligent as Harold Wincott can allow that doctors,*

24

## Business and Politics

Now, I too am bound to say that I cannot understand how a man as intelligent as Lord Campbell could so misunderstand the basic philosophy about profits which has consistently underlain my articles in *The Financial Times* over the long period I have been privileged to contribute to the paper.

Read again if you will what Lord Campbell has to say about the various responsibilities of management towards employees, customers and the community, as well as shareholders. Then read what I said on the same subject in an article here on 20 July 1965.

'The successful company', I wrote (and I'm quoting verbatim), 'is the company which gives equal weight to the interests of those who own it, those who work for it, those who buy its products, and if you like, the interests of the community at large. Indeed, I don't believe any company can succeed if it doesn't give equal weight to all these interests'.

So much for that. Lord Campbell also says he cannot understand how I can allow 'that doctors, teachers, civil servants, presumably financial journalists and so on may be influenced by moral, social and aesthetic considerations, while . . . businessmen can be motivated by greed for profit alone'.

On this, I would remind Lord Campbell of one particular point I have made in my articles on stock option schemes. I have always been opposed to such schemes precisely because they seek to create a specially privileged class among businessmen, and overlook the great contribution made to society by such people as doctors,

*teachers, civil servants, presumably financial journalists and so on may be influenced by moral social and aesthetic considerations; while he thinks that businessmen can be motivated by greed for profit alone. Men and women need food and drink and sex (not necessarily in that order); but no one urges that they should be intemperate in these and get the most they can from them at the expense of all else. Why should people be intemperate about profits? And anyway if they are, isn't it an open invitation to Trade Unions to be equally intemperate about wages?*

*Most businessmen are reasonably a-political. What worries and confuses them (us) most is lack of certainty about the intentions of Government – whether we like or dislike those intentions. I believe that Government and businessmen should stop involving themselves in these ideological semantics; but should concentrate on the vital need for efficient and productive businesses, making a proper return on capital employed (the return on capital employed is an essential yardstick of efficiency and productivity). Everybody in Britain can benefit from businesses which vigorously pursue and fulfil their responsibilities to shareholders, employees and customers; and everybody will lose from inefficient loss-making businesses.*

*The Government must decide the country's social and economic priorities. But, having done so, what we want from them is that they should expressly and consistently recognise the role of business in balanced terms – profits and all; and then positively help us to fulfil it.*

House of Lords                                                     CAMPBELL OF ESKAN teachers and civil servants (I don't know about financial journalists), without which contribution the specially privileged class of chaps stock option schemes seek to create could not exist. I may add that I know that my attitude towards such schemes has brought me into sharp conflict with some industrialists and people in the City.

In short, I would submit that Lord Campbell suggests that there are major differences between us which don't in fact exist. It follows that I can only say a hearty 'Hear-hear' to most of the rest of his letter.

But there *is* still a basic difference between us. Lord Campbell talks about 'ideological semantics'. (I never said a word about 'greed for profit alone' in my article last week.) He also talks about 'proper profits' and a 'proper return on capital'. Sir Frank Kearton in 1964 talked about the relationship which total company profits ought to bear to the national income.

Frankly, although I've been a financial journalist since 1930, I haven't a clue what constitutes a 'proper' profit or a 'proper' return on capital. And I don't think Sir Frank Kearton has a clue what relationship total company profits ought to bear to the national income. And even if he does, there isn't a damn thing he, as an individual industrialist, can do about it anyway.

So, say I, let Frank Kearton and Jock Campbell concentrate, within the broad principles on which we all agree, on earning the biggest profits they can.

Lord Campbell says that if companies don't produce an 'adequate' return on capital employed they won't be able to stay in business. This is a nice theory, but it just isn't true. Any competent investment analyst will produce example after example, and among our biggest companies at that, where, if we had up-to-date valuations of their assets, what the companies are earning would be less than the going rate of interest in the gilt-edged market.

Although I don't know what a proper return on capital is – and, of course, it must vary from industry to industry – I'm quite sure that what these companies are earning is an improper rate. And yet they bumble along, year in, year out, staying quite comfortably in business. And the major tax reform this Government has instituted has encouraged them to do precisely that; it has put the need to get the outside financial backing Lord Campbell refers to at a discount; it has put a premium on self-finance; so far as risk capital is concerned, it has largely removed the companies from the judgment of the market place.

## Business and Politics

Inevitably, I devoted a good deal of last week's article to the circumstances surrounding the abortive bid by ICI for Courtaulds. Let me recall some passages from an article I wrote here at that time, which was intended to underline the moral of the affair.

I said I didn't believe we should ever get out of our recurring troubles (this was in March, 1962) until we got a great deal closer to the American attitude towards profits. There, I pointed out, government is a good deal tougher towards monopoly than we are; there, profits, earned under much more competitive conditions, are regarded as a badge of honour, a measure of efficiency.

There – and this is very topical in to-day's context at home – 'economists bemoan the failure of corporate profits to rise in recent years because they know that so long as profits are sluggish so long will private investment, on which all growth and higher productivity depend, lag behind'. There, the trade unions urge management to get profits up, so that they can get their share of the increase.

Here, I pointed out, under every heading our attitudes are precisely the opposite. 'Not surprisingly, perhaps, in these conditions, many people think there is something shameful about profits, and seek euphemisms for the very word in company accounts'.

Ironically enough, I ended that article by urging the then Conservative Government to 'concentrate on establishing a really competitive economy, in which only the efficient can earn rising profits'. I pleaded with it to 'lead industry and the unions into schemes where among other things adequate compensation is paid to workers made redundant by modernisation'.

'Let it stop apologising', I concluded, 'for increased profits and dividends, and instead challenge the Socialists whenever they attempt to argue from false premises. Then, and then only, will Britain get out of its present state of stagnation'.

Well, times change and governments change. But the stagnation – and the message – remain. I don't apologise for or withdraw one word of last week's article. But I do urge men like Lord Campbell and Sir Frank Kearton, who have the ear of the present Government, to make a better job of educating Labour than I did with the Tories four and a-half years ago.

It will be a tough assignment, for quite a number of our present Ministers are on record, in public and private conversations and writings, to the effect that they don't believe in the profit motive, or profits. Some of them are now willing to concede that profits are necessary (even the Communists reached that conclusion some while ago) but they don't agree that profits belong to shareholders.

If Lord Campbell can hammer home to these men the altogether admirable views he expresses in the last two paragraphs of his letter, he will indeed have done this country an inestimable service.

# 2

## Business and the Public

# Capitalists, go home!

28 April 1959

AST week's questions in the House of Commons on American
investment in British industry afford a good opportunity for
discussion of an important subject. Very often the attitude
towards foreign investment is that it's jolly decent of the country at
the receiving end to allow the foreign capital in. And that unless said
foreign capital jolly well behaves itself it won't be allowed in; or,
if it's already there, it'll be nationalised pdq at the first sign of any
nonsense.

I'll not go into the question of the stupidity of a country which
happens itself to have investments all over the world adopting such
attitudes; or of what the average trade unionist here would say if –
as might happen – American capital in future by-passed this country
and went straight behind the tariff walls of the Common Market
countries instead. I'd just like to discuss the thing dispassionately as a
general proposition.

Now the first thing that strikes me as being a bit odd is that much of
the criticism of and the finger-wagging against immigrant capital
comes from people who are always urging the surplus countries of
the world to follow good creditor nation policies, which means
among other things investing part of their surpluses abroad. The
advice itself is sound enough. Indeed, one reason why the American
recession had surprisingly little effect abroad is that on the whole
America *has* followed good creditor policies and *has* been willing to
exchange part of her gold reserves for foreign investments. It seems a
little churlish, to say the least, then to turn round and cry: 'American
capitalists, go home'.

It would be naïve, however, to argue that American – and other –
capital goes venturing thousands of miles away from home out of
sheer altruism. Most industrial managements find it much easier,
much less troublesome, to invest at home. The truth is that it is the
rise of economic nationalism, the erection of tariff and quota barriers,
which have been the largest single factor in forcing companies to
establish plants overseas. And in America's case, the dollar shortage
in the post-war period, and more recently the desire to hedge against
Keynes's prediction that the US would become isolated as a high cost
producer, have certainly played their parts. But it is worth pondering

30

what the fate of consumers in many developing countries would have been had they been left to the mercies of infant and inefficient local producers. Any country really ought to be thankful for the capital and technical know-how immigrant capital brings.

Some of them are. Paradoxically enough, but very humanly, however, the more successful, the more beneficent immigrant capital proves itself, the more likely it is to run into trouble. For the locals tend to job backwards. They ignore the magnificent national assets which have been created and concentrate all their attention on the dividend remittances across the exchange, forgetting that it is axiomatic that the bigger these become the more good the investment is doing to the country concerned. They conveniently forget the failures and losses immigrant capital inevitably suffers from time to time. I know one multi-million plant in Australia which has been nothing but a headache to its owners from the word go. I would say that the majority of subsidiaries of UK companies in Canada have found that market one of the toughest in the world in which to get established.

None of this is to dispute – indeed I have argued on these lines myself for years – that it is in the interests of immigrant capital itself that investors in the receiving country should wherever possible be given a chance of participating in the equity of the 'foreign' business. Such a course is obviously wise and in the best interests of the parent company. On this, I would say that in my experience – and I don't think I'm being jingoistic in saying so – British companies do better than the Americans.

This was borne in on me again during my recent visit to South Africa, where you find the Ordinary shares of the subsidiaries or associates of AEI, Dorman Long, Ever Ready, Metal Box, Schweppes, Oldham and Son and Stewarts and Lloyds, for example, publicly quoted and owned by the South African public. In Australia, where the general tendency is for the individual States positively to compete for immigrant capital, and where it is freely admitted that the Holden car plant is an enormous asset to Australia, there is nevertheless some bitterness that every penny of the equity is owned by General Motors, and that all Australia has been allowed to put up is 'money' capital.

This sort of thing causes the pendulum to swing too violently. If local investors understandably enough take a dim view of being the Billy Muggins in an inflationary age in being allowed to put up only fixed-interest capital, Dr. M. S. Louw, the prominent Afrikaner financier and industrialist, surely goes too far in the opposite direction in urging overseas parent companies to decontrol their South African subsidiaries by making a majority shareholding available to South African investors. There is no compulsion, as I've said, on industrialists to invest abroad. If, having borne the heat and burden of the day in getting established, they are then required to sell out when the business is successfully established – and the local investors would not, of course, want to participate in the failures – they would keep their capital at home, to the great detriment of South Africa. When Mr Anton Rupert, chairman of the Rembrandt Tobacco Corporation, has got Carreras on its feet again, which is clearly going to take some doing, would it be reasonable to ask him to surrender control to UK investors? It would be interesting to have Dr Louw's views on that one.

Which brings me to my final point. There is a disposition, I think, to welcome foreign capital when it asks the mayor to turn the first sod in a green field site in the process of getting established, but to regard it as slightly smelly and indecent when it buys its way into an established undertaking. 'Many members', said Mr Harold Wilson in the House last week, 'probably draw a sharp distinction between American investment in this country, which brings new firms, factories, techniques and know-how, and the purchase of shares, which may lead to the control of an important British firm by alien ownership.'

Really, this cock isn't a very efficient fighter. The Americans – or anyone else – can get control of a vital British interest, if they've got the know-how, by starting from scratch just as easily (if not so cheaply) as by buying into an existing concern. If they've got the know-how, they can do just as good a job for the receiving economy by taking over an established business; indeed, if they resuscitate an inefficient business they may be doing a better job.

Of course, they may tread on managerial corns, or provide individual shareholders with a handsome capital profit in the process, which is why you get the oddest companions in the chorus of protest which such deals arouse. But we had better be grown-up in considering this matter. The free movement of capital is too important in the common interest to allow either vested interests or the yearnings of the Socialists for complete State-ownership of our industry to stop it happening.

# Should we paddle our own welfare canoes?

23 July 1963

---

'They [the Conservatives in opposition] could examine the indiscriminate nature of so much of our social services which all too often perpetuates poverty and hands out unneeded largesse.' – This column, 9 July.

---

THE Institute of Economic Affairs is to be congratulated on its enterprise in commissioning Mass-Observation to inquire into the extent of the British people's knowledge of and preference for state and private provision for education, health services and pensions. The basic thinking which set the inquiry in motion was this: that despite the admitted imperfections of the free market – imperfections which it should be government's unceasing task to remedy – the consumer's machinery of choice to-day 'is at least in working order' everywhere – except in the field of social welfare.

Here, until now, there has been little evidence to show whether the public really gets what it wants. It may be that all it gets is what the politicians think it wants; and the snag, and a very topical snag it could be to-day, is that the electorate more often than not votes *against* things rather than *for* things.

This isn't to say that very substantial sections of the community don't want public welfare publicly provided – no one who remembers the response to the Beveridge Report of 1942 would dispute that. It is to say that our approach to the problem of public welfare hitherto has ignored two things.

First, there is the fact that there will always be a minority which can and would rather make its own provision for hardship and betterment; and secondly, that in a prosperous community, the size of that minority must be constantly increasing – although it would be quite wrong to assume that this minority consists exclusively of wealthy or better off people.

There are other good reasons why a new look at welfare would be timely. Granted that the public welcome to the Beveridge Report

33

was overwhelming, it is not unimportant to recall that the report itself assumed a general level of unemployment of 8½ per cent in the post-war years. We would have had a very different report – and a very different public response – if Lord Beveridge had been at work in the post-war conditions we have actually seen, with an average level of unemployment only a quarter of the rate he assumed.

Again, there is the dawning realisation that in the country which became known throughout the world just after the war – because of Beveridge – as 'the Welfare State', provision for hardship and betterment has in fact lagged a good deal behind what is done in countries which only a decade or so ago were regarded as citadels of reaction. Significantly enough, much of what these countries do in the way of social security is the responsibility of the private and not the public sector.

There are also the broader economic implications of our policy. Since 1938, the proportion of our national income devoted to social service expenditure has risen from 11 to 18 per cent; government social services now account for almost half total government expenditure. In other directions, the public sector has been assuming increasingly important proportions since the middle fifties, and, in the light of the immense tasks which still need to be tackled in that sector, radical measures will be necessary if the trend is to be halted, let alone reversed.

Whether one regards this expansion of the public sector as a good thing or a bad, in a philosophical sense, I don't think there can be much dispute that it tends to increase inflationary pressures, the preemption of resources, public borrowing and the level of taxation, all of which militate against the prosperity of the private sector on which, in the ultimate resort, the viability of the public sector itself rests. It is not so much a matter of possibly sawing through the branch on which we all sit; the ultimate danger is to the tree itself, root and branch. Is it altogether a coincidence that the countries which rely on the private sector to provide much welfare, to the benefit of the public purse, have made the greatest economic progress?

The Institute of Economic Affairs itself puts the economic aspects of welfare thus: 'Economists concerned with efficiency rather than political expediency must examine the consequences of political decisions in the use of large amounts of resources and explore new methods of learning whether the assumptions made about public preferences are well founded.'

34

To those who know the Institute, and its philosophy, these words are very significant. We can be quite sure that the Institute, with its well-known predilection for a free society, will be accused on the strength of this inquiry of wanting to dismantle the Welfare State. But in fact, all that the present inquiry is concerned with is an attempt to get at the truth as to what the public itself would prefer.

The distilled essence of the results of the inquiry – which was in fact very detailed, with sub-divisions for income groups and political allegiances – are shown in my graph. ('Status quo' is convenient if misleading shorthand, for in each case the question envisaged that the state would provide better cover and services as we grow more prosperous. 'Don't knows' – never more than 2 per cent – are represented by the black slivers).

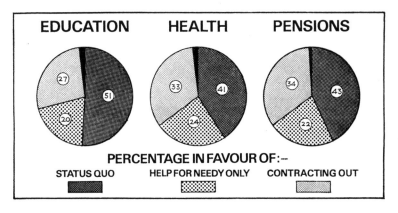

The Institute of Economic Affairs itself is obviously anxious that its inquiry should be seen only as a 'preliminary effort in a neglected field'. It acknowledges that since most people have little or no experience of making a choice between state and private services, it was not always easy to present some of the possible alternatives in simple terms. It admits that there may have been uncertainties in the questions and ambiguities in the answers.

It is also quite clear in each case that a substantial number of those questioned would prefer – and presumably with good reason – that the State should continue to provide these basic social services and on an expanding scale and even at the cost of higher taxes. Equally, however, the Institute seems justified in claiming that it is inescapable that 'people are apparently more receptive to the idea of radical reform in welfare than is commonly supposed'.

It seems unlikely, on the record, that the Labour Party would be willing to consider the recasting of our social welfare system to provide only for those in need and to allow other people to pay their own way and, in consequence, to enjoy lower taxation.

Mind you, if Mr Wilson is really out to court 'the striving classes', he ought to take notice of this inquiry's findings. For 44 per cent of those interviewed declared themselves to be Labour sympathisers, against only 24 per cent for the Tories and 14 per cent for the Liberals, and substantial minorities of the Labour supporters favoured some freedom of choice, particularly for health services and pensions. Still, I can't really see Mr Wilson carrying a banner at the next election proclaiming 'Labour Will Set You Free to Provide Your Own Pension'.

It seems equally unlikely that the Tories, having had nearly 12 years (of increasing affluence) in office, can ever take time off from the other chores of government to sit back and look objectively at this whole question. But in opposition they might, on the evidence of this inquiry, subsequently find a surprising amount of support for a new deal which could provide better state welfare where it is needed and less where it can be furnished privately.

# New look at the World Company League

31 December 1963

THIS article is, if you like, a continuation of the series which started here towards the end of 1962. The series began with some calculations attempting to show the relative performances of equities in various countries in real terms, which calculations were derived from the deflation of share indexes by the respective cost of living indexes. Whether one took the mid-thirties or an early post-war year as a base, the results were, to say the least, unflattering to Britain, even when allowance is made for such factors as our high interest rates in the late fifties and early sixties. In broad (and real) terms, and to take the comparison there can be least argument about,

*The Financial Times* index of 30 industrials shows virtually no appreciation since the middle thirties, whereas the Dow Average of the
same number of US industrials has risen about $2\frac{1}{2}$ times.

The comparisons were so surprising that I later went on to produce
some figures which to my mind at least went a long way towards
explaining the poor performance in real terms of our leading Ordinary
shares. These figures included, for example, international comparisons of sales per employee, net profit as a percentage on sales and as a
percentage on assets; and (based on *Fortune's* annual survey) the
amount of assets various companies in different countries put
behind each worker. On each count, most of the British companies
examined were lagging behind their international competitors.

These exercises aroused a good deal of interest, not only in this
country but all over the world; they were indeed prodded along by
letters received from readers in the most unlikely places. This particular article is in that tradition; the table which accompanies it came
originally from a chap in Canada whose real work is concerned with
international economics but who is also interested in 'hard' investment matters.

The table speaks for itself but nevertheless some comments on
the figures are called for. The figures are all percentages, with net
profits and depreciation aggregated in the last columns to provide
what is called 'Cash Flow'. (To be purist, it is gross cash flow in the
sense that the profits are shown before dividend payments.) The
percentages are percentages of what we may call Ordinary shareholders' funds – subscribed capital plus reserves attributable to the
equity.

I am indebted to various brokers both here and in America for
checking those of the figures I was not able to check myself. Even so,
various reservations have to be made, particularly about the German
and Japanese companies. The German figures are, frankly, estimates.
They have to be, because with German companies in this sort of
exercise profit is largely built up by taking tax provisions as a starting
point; moreover, profits are not consolidated and Ordinary shareholders' funds often include contingent reserves which in the judgment of investment analysts represent merely conservative accounting
and would, in a show-down, be found to belong to the equity. There is
also the general feeling that German companies are undercapitalised
(in shareholders' funds) by 'Anglo-Saxon' standards. If this is true, the

37

## THE COUNTRIES COMPARED

| | Net profits 1962 1961 % | | Depreciation 1962 1961 % | | Cash flow 1962 1961 | |
|---|---|---|---|---|---|---|
| **Germany** | | | | | | |
| Volkswagen | 26.4 | 20.1 | 21.4 | 25.3 | 47.8 | 45.4 |
| Daimler Benz | 24.9 | 27.2 | 21.0 | 24.1 | 45.9 | 51.3 |
| Demag | 13.9 | 16.0 | 7.0 | 8.6 | 20.9 | 24.6 |
| Bayer | 12.6 | 15.2 | 14.3 | 17.2 | 26.9 | 32.4 |
| Thyssen | 9.7 | 11.1 | 15.5 | 17.4 | 25.2 | 28.5 |
| Mannesmann | 10.4 | 13.9 | 13.9 | 14.2 | 24.3 | 28.1 |
| Siemens | 12.2 | 14.2 | 21.1 | 19.8 | 33.3 | 34.0 |
| **United States** | | | | | | |
| General Motors | 21.7 | 14.6 | 6.7 | 6.8 | 28.4 | 21.4 |
| Ford Motor | 14.1 | 13.1 | 11.6 | 12.6 | 25.7 | 25.7 |
| US Steel | 4.7 | 5.6 | 9.2 | 7.2 | 13.9 | 12.8 |
| Allied Chemical | 9.5 | 10.3 | 12.2 | 10.7 | 21.7 | 21.0 |
| Monsanto Chemical | 10.9 | 10.6 | 13.5 | 13.3 | 24.4 | 23.9 |
| Dow Chemical | 9.3 | 9.9 | 13.8 | 13.8 | 23.1 | 23.7 |
| IBM | 17.5 | 17.5 | 20.1 | 21.0 | 37.6 | 38.5 |
| General Electric | 15.7 | 15.4 | 7.5 | 7.5 | 23.2 | 22.9 |
| Blaw Knox | 4.9 | 6.6 | 4.5 | 4.2 | 9.4 | 10.8 |
| Utd. Engineering | 8.6 | 12.6 | 5.5 | 3.6 | 14.1 | 16.2 |
| **Japan** | | | | | | |
| Shin. Mitsubishi Heavy Industries | 10.2 | 12.0 | 13.8 | 14.0 | 24.0 | 26.0 |
| Toyota Motor | 15.0 | 14.5 | 16.0 | 14.5 | 31.0 | 29.0 |
| Tokyo Shibaura El. | 11.5 | 12.3 | 9.5 | 9.8 | 21.0 | 22.1 |
| Hitachi | 10.5 | 13.5 | 14.3 | 13.8 | 24.8 | 27.3 |
| Yawata Iron & Steel | 3.0 | 11.0 | 16.8 | 16.5 | 19.8 | 27.5 |
| Mitsubishi Chemical | 10.3 | 10.8 | 14.3 | 17.3 | 24.6 | 28.1 |
| Fuji Iron and Steel | 3.0 | 6.8 | 13.0 | 13.3 | 16.0 | 20.1 |
| **UK** | | | | | | |
| ICI | 5.9 | 5.5 | 7.5 | 7.0 | 13.4 | 12.5 |
| Elliott-Automation | 12.2 | 10.3 | 6.5 | 5.6 | 18.6 | 15.9 |
| Stewarts and Lloyds | 5.6 | 7.1 | 5.0 | 5.0 | 10.6 | 12.1 |
| BMC | 12.1 | 4.4 | 9.5 | 8.7 | 21.6 | 13.1 |
| Guest Keen | 5.6 | 6.0 | 6.5 | 6.2 | 12.1 | 12.2 |
| Vickers | 5.1 | 4.5 | 3.8 | 3.5 | 8.9 | 8.0 |
| United Steel | 5.3 | 8.8 | 5.4 | 5.5 | 10.7 | 14.3 |
| AEI | 3.0 | 2.4 | 5.0 | 5.1 | 8.0 | 7.5 |

*The above table expresses net profits before equity dividends, and depreciation, as percentages of equity shareholders' funds and aggregates these figures into a (gross) percentage 'cash flow'.*

German percentages may be unfairly high compared with those figures for the US and the UK.

A complication in the case of Japan is that many companies there apparently don't consolidate subsidiary results with those of the parent, which may lead either to over- or under-statement of the true results depending on the fortunes of the subsidiaries. The figures for two Japanese companies which do consolidate – Fuji Iron and Steel and Hitachi – seem, however, to fit in reasonably well with the others.

With all these reservations, it is the order of magnitude which counts. Broadly speaking, the foreign companies seem to earn profits on shareholders' funds and to provide depreciation on double the scale that our companies do; in particular, they seem to put aside a good deal more for depreciation. Can we wonder, on this showing, that the performance of British equities, divested of the inflationary element, has been relatively so poor?

In detail, too, the figures are fascinating. There is in America the contrast between an 'old' and (in recent years) under-employed business like United States Steel and the 'new' and vigorously expanding International Business Machines. There is the tremendous improvement in the British Motor Corporation figures (the latest of which relates to the year ended 31 July 1963) showing what a transformation full capacity operations and heavy investment can make. The Elliott-Automation figures, too, seem to point a similar moral.

Pondering over the figures, I couldn't help drawing several morals from them. First, must all the politicians and trade unionists and others go on talking, parrot-like, about the need to keep profits here down when so far as one can see they are already too low? And, secondly, arising out of this, wouldn't it be a splendid thing if some professional or learned body – maybe Neddy itself – got down to a meticulous examination of figures such as these and the others I have noted earlier in this series of articles, first to confirm that these apparently serious discrepancies do exist, and secondly, if they do, to put on public record some authoritative explanation of why foreign companies do so much better.

So far as one can judge, the system of taxing company profits doesn't vary very much in the advanced economies these days. Is the burden and the means of raising other taxation something which holds us back? Is industrial plant operated more fully, is there more shift-working, in countries like the United States, Germany and Japan? If so, is this why they provide so much more for depreciation than our companies do? Is industry in these countries more competitive, are there fewer restrictive practices all round, among labour and management, is there less protection, to explain why their companies are more profitable and therefore presumably, by definition, more efficient?

If Neddy could get down to this job, it would, I suggest, be the most valuable contribution it could make towards the full restoration of our fortunes. For, whatever our political beliefs, we may as well get one thing straight. The private sector is the foundation on which all else in the modern economy rests. So far as revenue raising or direct exports are concerned, the public sector, on the whole, is literally a dead loss. And yet, as recent developments on so many fronts suggests, and as indeed everyone agrees, that public sector must be considerably expanded. Can we build that considerably expanded public sector on the foundations of a private sector which doesn't seem to be nearly as efficient as it should – or, on the example of its competitors, could be?

# Never the twain shall meet

30 March 1965

IN October, 1958 (so help me, this is a true story) a journalist I know found himself in a jolly embarrassing position. He went to speak at a seminar for 'senior management'. A certain distinguished economist had also been invited to read a paper.

The economist spoke first, before lunch. Imagine the consternation of the journalist as he discovered that through some misunderstanding both he and the economist had prepared papers on the same subject – with a title something like 'Britain's Economic Future'; imagine his horror as he further discovered that practically everything he proposed to say was in flat contradiction to what the distinguished economist was even then saying.

The sequel was better than it might have been. The economist couldn't stay after lunch. The journalist put a new title on his talk, which he otherwise left as it was. The audience, and the sponsors of the conference, seemed reasonably happy with both papers. Of course, it *was* a good lunch.

If it was variety the customers were after, this happy outcome wasn't surprising. The economist said that if we were to avoid 1 million unemployed over the ensuing 12 months we must have at least £500 million of new orders, secured not through wage increases (which would only push up prices and therefore not really increase demand) but, so far as the journalist understood, through plain deficit financing. You don't need to be told, do you, exactly what the journalist said?

Who proved right? Alas and alack, we shall never know. The journalist could claim that the seasonally adjusted figure for unemployment fell from 524,000 around the time of the conference to 509,000 by April, 1959, which hardly suggested the 1 million was coming up over the next six months. But in that month the Budget for 1959–60 aimed at an increase in the overall deficit of £539 million. This was just what the economist ordered, with a bit extra thrown in for good measure, although in fact the actual increase in the overall deficit that year turned out 12 months later to be 'only' £314 million.

The economist, however, could argue that without that deficit, we *should* have seen unemployment at 1 million. What we do know is that, so far from going there, with the aid of the increased deficit unemployment in fact went on falling virtually without a pause until it got down to 302,000 in June, 1961. And we all know what happened then. At least, Mr Selwyn Lloyd does.

I was reminded of this story the other day as I was doing my reading. There was Professor Frank Paish, at it again, in a scholarly article in the *Statist*. Jim Callaghan, said Professor Paish, had three alternatives. First, a do-nothing, 'anti-capitalist' Budget, which would mean another major crisis pdq. Secondly, increase taxes on the general public by £200 million, which would help but not do the job properly. Finally, a still heavier check to consumption, which would stop its rise completely and very likely push private investment down later on, whereupon the credit squeeze should be relaxed and the tax on company profits cut.

There was Sir Roy Harrod, at it again, in a scholarly market review. Saying: 'It is to be hoped that the new Department for Economic Affairs will safeguard the Cabinet from the error of supposing that, when in doubt, it is better to play for safety, namely – to aim at a high ratio of revenue to expenditure'. Adding 'it would be very dangerous to bring about a situation in which unemployment began to rise again'. Pleading that 'any further reduction in the increase of consumer expenditures would endanger the aggregate demand falling below the level needed for full growth'.

Jolly interesting, isn't it? I'm not criticising either of these distinguished gentlemen, of course. I'm just saying that if you'll name 'em – politicians, economists or financial journalists – I'll tell you what sort of Budget they think we ought to have. Christian names will do, although, of course, you'll have to say which Harold, which George, and which Nigel you have in mind.

You could play the game in America, too. Remember the intellectual scrap a few years back between Doctors Arthur Burns and Walter Heller? Dr Heller it was who argued that the United States was wasting thousands of millions of dollars worth of goods and services because its productive capacity wasn't being fully employed. Dr Burns it was who had his doubts.

Thinking back on that episode, and remembering the way the American economy has steamed ahead since, it seemed to me that in the United States at least this old, old dispute between the expansionists and the economic conservatives had been settled once and for all – and in favour of Dr Heller. Then I re-read an article I'd written here in August, 1961, on the Burns-Heller confrontation and found that Dr Burns' caution was based on fears 'that the Kennedy programme must endanger the recent price stability, lead to a decline in the export surplus, and revive fears for the dollar and expectations of a gold price increase'!

Shall we ever find out who's right and who's wrong in this country? We might, if either school got a clear run for a long enough period to prove its thesis. But that presupposes that the Paish school's run starts soon enough after a general election, and that the Government has a comfortable enough majority, so that the medicine has time to work and to produce results, say, 18 months before the next election.

I know that journalist I was telling you about at the beginning of this article didn't believe there was the slightest chance that unemployment would rise to 1 million before October, 1959, £500 million of printed money or no £500 million. But the run wasn't long enough for the Tory Government to take a chance that the journalist might have been right and the economist wrong.

## Business and the Public

There was a general election in October, 1959, you may remember, and Harold Macmillan with his memories of Stockton-on-Tees in the thirties, wasn't taking any chances. Maybe if he had, the Tories would have won in both 1959 and 1964, but that, like everything else in this article, is pure conjecture.

Equally, it seems unlikely, our balance of payments position and reserves being what they are, that the Harrod school will get a long enough run to prove *its* case. The Harrod run, in the circumstances, would be rather like driving a racing car at top speed round the edge of the cliffs at Beachy Head – a most stimulating and exciting experience, but a bit trying on the nerves.

If it were only our nerves which were involved, maybe the old tag about l'Anglais avec son même sang-froid would be relevant. But the chaps across the Channel would also be watching the performance through their binoculars, and I rather doubt whether their nerves would be equal to the strain.

So my bet would be that the two schools go on stating their case with all their customary lucidity and persuasion, and without gaining a single convert; but that, come 6 April, we shall find that the thing hasn't been put to the test; that somehow a compromise will be reached between the chaps at the one end of the corridor in Great George Street who don't have to worry about the figures, and the chaps at the other end who do.

Well, we've survived on compromises for a long while now, and I don't doubt we'll survive the one I expect to see to-day week. Meanwhile, the economic expansionists and the economic conservatives will continue their debate, and jolly interesting reading it will all make. And, of course, each school will remain absolutely convinced that if only its ideas *were* put to the test they would be triumphantly vindicated.

# An amateur sociologist reports

IT was a jolly interesting letter; so interesting that I thought I ought to tell you about it. I don't know the fellow who wrote it. You won't find him in the Directory of Directors or Who's Who. He seems to be just an ordinary chap, with an extraordinary interest in what goes on in the district where he lives, which is in the heart of the industrial midlands.

His theme? Industrial productivity, and why it isn't rising. 'The main reason in the Midlands', he writes, 'is that the Affluent Society has created many men who can well afford to take days off and can still be well off.

'Many of these men are not slightly interested in prestige, and unlike the middle classes are not always striving for a better house in a better district with a better car and continental holidays, etc. They are quite content to live in a subsidised council flat or house, have a few drinks in the local or at the club, have a game of Bingo or a night at the greyhound track. They can do this easily and still have plenty of money to spare.

'I know plenty of workers (in two specified Midlands towns) who have a few thousands in the bank but you would not get them to buy a £4,000 house. They would rather let their money earn them some interest and live in a council house. No £1-a-week rates and a further 30s maintenance costs for them. This may be short-sighted but it is true.

'My own friend works as a clicker at a local firm and his wife works [in a factory], too. The total income is never less than £50 a week. He will take a month off sick in the new year and, with his sick pay from the union, NHI pay, and his tax refunds, he will net £14 for that time. Their rent [in a new council estate] is 43s and he would no more think of buying a house than trying to fly.

'Many families have incomes of £60 a week. They buy an inexpensive car and live reasonably well but their average way of life still enables them to have money to spare. If taxation were to be reduced these people would have even more incentive to have a few days off. My experience seems to indicate that the only time a man will really graft is when he has nothing in his pocket, but if conditions are created that give high earnings to people who are content to live in a moderate sort of way, then more and more people will take a little more time off and draw a little bit more off the Welfare State.

'The bus workers [in a nearby town] expect to get £1,000 a year for a 40-hour week in the near future. Three engineers from the local firm have told me that when this comes about they are changing their jobs. If the service industries pay attractive money we shall see some movement out of the factories to join the ever-increasing number of non-productive workers. I thought it should be the other way round.

'I have just been talking to a motor engineer. He says his wage for four nights' work is £29 gross. He has not been in on a Friday night shift since the boycott of this shift started. He also said his wage gave him a good standard of living, and he would not have gone in on a Friday night if the wages for that shift were tax-free. Incidentally, he lives in a council house and he has been off work (sickness) for seven weeks.

'At the hospital here, employees are allowed three days off without a sick certificate, provided the hospital is informed. Everything from women spring-cleaning to men painting and decorating is done [on 'sick leave']. I know of one man recently having two weeks off to do his bathroom tiling. Makes you think, doesn't it?'

It certainly does. You'll not find the reader's testimony confirmed in any official figures from the Ministry of Labour that I know of. But you'll find some supporting evidence for what he says in the fact that, since full employment was reached by the end of 1964, the index of industrial production has been as flat as a pancake below its peak. And I don't think Lord Robens, with his miner who worked four days a week because he couldn't earn enough in three, would dispute much of my correspondent's tale.

I would suggest, however, that it is a matter which we ought to consider quite dispassionately, not least those who *are* in the Directory of Directors and who also sometimes put leisure and, these days, even early retirement, first. Admittedly, motives may differ. Whereas the reader's chaps would work less if taxation were reduced, there must be many at the other end of the income scale who calculate how little, in terms of net income, a hiving off of gross income involves these days, and take appropriate action.

Moreover, if those whose work is challenging and stimulating take the odd day off (have you ever been to Lord's on week-days when a Test match is played there, or Ascot, or the Varsity rugby match?)

can we really criticise those whose work is dull and repetitive and boring in the extreme when, as my correspondent says, 'conditions are created that give high earnings to people who are content to live in a moderate sort of way'.

If my correspondent is right, it is indeed difficult to know what we can do about it. Given a $98\frac{1}{2}$ per cent employed economy, it's not much use sacking the chap who spent his 'sick-leave' tiling the bathroom. When he'd fixed the last tile, he could take his pick of half-a-dozen other jobs, possibly better paid than the one at the hospital. If you cut his tax, he'd probably be 'sick' three weeks next year.

About the only thing you can do, I submit, is to create conditions fundamentally different from those my correspondent describes, and which we all know exist to-day. And what fascinated me about his letter was that I received it at precisely the moment of time when it is becoming more and more evident that this Government of ours has not the slightest intention of altering the conditions my chap describes.

I was commenting last week on one thing we can be sure George Brown and Jim Callaghan agree about these days – that a measure of unemployment is no answer to our economic difficulties. On top of this, as we also saw here last week, official wage rates have meant less and less in recent years, and all sorts of inducements are being added to rising amounts of take-home pay to seduce people from one factory to another.

While this is going on, prices of everyday necessities, from bread to coal, are being held down, thus increasing the net worth of the pay packet. Rents, we can be sure, will either be cut or held lower than the economic level by Mr Crossman's new Act.

And, in the Queen's Speech, we have the undertaking to provide still more of the council houses which our chap in the Midlands reckons constitute such a disincentive to workers there. Throw in for good measure the further promise of subsidised mortgage rates to the exceptions who prove my correspondent's alleged rule that his friends prefer council houses and you've got practically every ingredient you need to put a still higher premium on the pursuit of leisure.

This Government is a great employer of academics. It's a great believer in National Plans, Little Neddies, and so on. Would it not be sensible if it employed a professional sociologist to conduct a survey of British attitudes towards work and leisure in the Affluent Society; to bring up-to-date Richard Hoggart's work in 'The Uses of Literacy', which was done, after all, in the early 'fifties; to confirm or refute what my correspondent says these attitudes are?

For if my chap's right, all the good work National Plans, Little Neddies and so on could do looks like being frustrated not only by what is going on now but by the accentuation of what is going on now which must result from developing Government policy, admirable though that policy may seem to be on humanitarian grounds.

Alternatively, since it seems the Opposition is coming to believe that those who can afford to pay economic prices for goods and services ought to pay them, and that only the really needy should be assisted by the State; and that any savings should be used to encourage the people in the Directory of Directors to stay away from Lord's, Ascot and Twickenham, or not to retire early, it might be worth Mr Heath's while to pay for a similar, independent piece of research.

Clearly, someone ought to.

# 3

## Profits and Productivity

# The £604,000,000 that gets away from 2,000 companies

18 June 1963

I HAVE got sufficiently involved with some international comparisons myself to know how qualified such comparisons have to be. I brooded a good deal, therefore, over the comparative figures, on 'Sales per Employee' and 'Net Profit after tax as per cent of Sales and of Assets', which appear in the booklet Mr F. R. Bentley has produced and which I mentioned here last week, before writing this article.

I am satisfied the figures do stand in need of some qualification, although these qualifications work both ways. In calculating the 'sales per employee' figures, the official rates of exchange have, of course, been used. I always mistrust the $2.80-£ rate in such comparisons between Britain and America.

The United States is a 'high-price' country. This doesn't matter internally, for high wages match high prices: you remember the classic calculation that about the only thing the American has to work more hours to buy than his opposite number here is a haircut. But I think I would use a bigger divisor than 2.80 to convert sale per US employee when comparing them with British, Common Market or Japanese sales.

Secondly, my accountant friends who know America tell me that revaluation of assets is much frowned on there: indeed, the Americans may write down their assets more speedily than we do. This may mean that the figures expressing American companies' profits as a percentage of assets are flatteringly high. (I'm bound to add, however, that there aren't many British companies in the table which have revalued their assets.)

On the other hand, to the extent to which companies in the Common Market countries understate their profits in their published accounts in a way British and American companies don't, *their* figures of profits as a percentage of sales and assets will be too modest.

With all these reservations, however, I don't think it can be disputed that the figures on the whole provide some additional evidence that British industry could do a good deal better than it does, and that the comparisons go some way at least towards explaining the relatively poor performance of our industrial equities.

## Profits and Productivity

The British companies in the tables you will see are anonymous. I think this is understandable. You can feel you have a duty to draw attention to a national problem – which this is – without crying stinking fish and pillorying particular enterprises. Anyway, any reasonably competent investment analyst would unearth the identity of the British companies in a couple of hours, given the accounts and his slide rule. One final point. Space considerations have precluded me from quoting all Mr Bentley's examples. But I don't think my selections are unfair.

### SOME COMPARISONS OF PROFITABILITY

| | STEEL | | | | CARS | | |
|---|---|---|---|---|---|---|---|
| US | a | b | c | | a | b | c |
| US Steel | 5.9 | 5.8 | 3.7 | Gnl. Mtrs. | 7.4 | 7.8 | 10.1 |
| Bethlehem | 5.7 | 6.0 | 5.3 | Ford | 9.1 | 6.1 | 8.0 |
| Inland | 9.3 | 7.6 | 6.5 | Chrysler | 10.2 | 0.5 | 0.8 |
| **Foreign** | | | | | | | |
| Mannesmann | 3.8 | 2.8 | 3.2 | VW | 5.7 | 3.7 | 6.9 |
| Aug. Thyssen | 5.7 | 2.2 | 2.5 | Fiat | 3.4 | 4.1 | 2.7 |
| Fugi | 5.4 | 4.0 | 2.2 | Citroen | 4.1 | 0.7 | 1.6 |
| **UK** | | | | | | | |
| 1 | 4.3 | 3.1 | 4.2 | 1 | 4.0 | 1.9 | 3.8 |
| 2 | 2.7 | 4.7 | 4.4 | 2 | 2.8 | 3.2 | 3.3 |
| 3 | 3.2 | 4.5 | 3.5 | | | | |
| 4 | 4.9 | 3.7 | 2.3 | | | | |

| | ELECTRICAL | | | | CHEMICALS, FIBRES | | | | RUBBER | | |
|---|---|---|---|---|---|---|---|---|---|---|---|
| US | a | b | c | | a | b | c | | a | b | c |
| Gnl. Elec. | 6.4 | 5.4 | 8.9 | Du Pont | 9.1 | 18.8 | 12.5 | Goodyear | 5.7 | 5.2 | 6.8 |
| W'house | 6.2 | 2.4 | 3.0 | U. Carbide | 9.5 | 9.1 | 8.2 | Firestone | 5.1 | 5.4 | 7.1 |
| RCA | 6.5 | 2.3 | 3.8 | Monsanto | 8.8 | 7.4 | 6.0 | US Rbr. | 5.8 | 2.9 | 4.1 |
| **Foreign** | | | | | | | | | | | |
| Phillips | 2.1 | 6.6 | 5.2 | Hoechst | 4.9 | 4.4 | 4.2 | Pirelli | 3.6 | 3.6 | 3.5 |
| AEG | 2.0 | 2.2 | 2.7 | Rhone-P | 4.6 | 2.5 | 2.5 | Michelin | 4.1 | 1.0 | 8.3 |
| ASEA | 3.3 | 3.1 | 3.1 | Snia Visc. | 3.0 | 6.6 | 6.5 | | | | |
| **UK** | | | | | | | | | | | |
| 1 | 2.0 | 1.6 | 1.4 | 1 | 4.8 | 5.9 | 3.7 | 1 | 2.8 | 2.2 | 3.0 |
| 2 | 2.5 | 1.1 | 1.3 | 2 | 2.9 | 5.5 | 3.5 | | | | |
| 3 | 1.7 | 0.9 | 0.8 | | | | | | | | |

*The table is based on 1961 figures ; 'a' represents sales per employee (£'000) ; 'b' net profit after tax as % on sales ; 'c' net profit after tax as % of assets.*

Well now, let's revert to the results of the 2,000–odd publicly quoted manufacturing companies between the years 1950 and 1961. The sample of companies presumably changes, and the most recent figures are based on a smaller sample than that taken in 1950. Let's strike an average, therefore, for 1950 and 1961. We find that the average company in 1950 employed net assets of £1,558,000 to earn a net income of £349,000 (22.4 per cent). The average company in 1961 employed £7,390,000 of net assets to earn a net income of £980,000 (13.3 per cent).

The average company in 1961 was therefore employing £5,832,000 more assets to produce £631,000 more income (10.8 per cent). The profitability of the new capital employed by this average company was thus less than half the profitability of the capital it was employing in 1950.

This is a pretty shattering state of affairs. There can be no doubt that conditions were a lot more favourable for profit-making in 1950 than they are to-day. There is plenty of evidence in fact that American industry has gone through a somewhat similar phase of reduced profitability.

But there can be no doubt that the energies of the nation in general and management in particular ought to be concentrated on recapturing say one-half of the profitability the average company lost over these 12 years. Let's suppose the average company in 1961 had earned 16 per cent on the £5,832,000 of extra assets (compared with 1950) it was employing. Then, instead of earning £631,000 extra income, it would have earned £933,000 more, a difference of £302,000.

If you have 2,000 companies earning £302,000 extra income, the country is £604,000,000 better off and, of course, there are far many more companies in Britain than 2,000. But even £604,000,000 is an awful lot of money to be forgoing each year. Think how happy the Chancellor would be. Think how much better off shareholders and workers and everyone would be if it existed. Think where the FT Industrial index would be standing.

Positively mouth-watering, isn't it? Personally, I've no doubt it could be done, if we all got down to it, pulled our fingers out and so on. Why, compare the Courtaulds of 1961 with the Courtaulds of 1963, and you get some idea of the possibilities. (Maybe we should hire Paul Chambers to go round making other bids.)*

Me, I don't think you'll do it by talking about productivity. Go out in the street and ask ten people to tell you the difference between

*A reference to the unsuccessful bid for Courtaulds by ICI.

production and productivity and you'll be lucky if you get one who can. But everyone knows what the words profits and profitability mean. They may not (some of them) like the words. But explain to them what we could do with this (minimum) of £604,000,000 a year and maybe profit will cease to be a dirty word. That'll be the day, my word.


# The 4½ per cent truth about Capitalism

28 April 1964

WHATEVER the calendar may say, statistically this is the season of mists and mellow fruitfulness. I propose in this and next week's articles to use some of the latest official crop of statistics to clear away some of the mists (or are they smoke-screens?) which have enveloped our debates recently. This week, I want to return to the question of the profits and profitability of British industry.

The point is, of course, that so much of the Opposition's case in the Budget debate centred on the manner in which, it was alleged, the rise in profits and dividends had outstripped the rise in wages, and how companies were paying out less and less in taxation and individuals more and more.

A great deal depends, as we all know, on the base date you choose for such exercises. Companies have undoubtedly been pushing dividends up recently, largely against the eventuality of a Labour government coming to power. It would thus suit Labour to take a quite recent base to make political capital out of a sense of unease the party itself has created. This is fair enough, in a political context, but no investment analyst would trust the recent trend very far.

Equally, you can take one particular series of figures going back over a longer period, and these would seem to make your case. Thus Messrs Wilson, Callaghan and Jay, in the budget debate, were all arguing that dividends had increased unconscionably; that companies were paying a smaller percentage of their profits away in taxation; and were urging, more generally, not just that profits

# The Business of Capitalism

should be more heavily taxed but that the level of indirect taxation ought to be reduced, not increased.

It so happens that we have a pretty complete record on all this, going back to 1950. Each year, the Board of Trade 'processes' the financial results of a large sample (of between 2,000 and 3,000 public quoted companies) of British manufacturing and distributing industry. My table gives the highlights of the annual profit and loss account of what is, very nearly, 'British Industry Ltd'.

## WHAT THE ACCOUNTS SHOW

£m. (*Percentage of Total in Brackets*)

| | Gross Income | Ord. and Pref. Divds. | Interest on long-term loans | Taxation | Depreciation and other provs. | Retained in reserves |
|---|---|---|---|---|---|---|
| 1950 | 1,316 | 307 (*23.3*) | 18 (*1.4*) | 443 (*33.7*) | 192 (*14.6*) | 356 (*27.1*) |
| 1951 | 1,544 | 321 (*20.8*) | 22 (*1.4*) | 585 (*37.9*) | 211 (*13.7*) | 404 (*26.2*) |
| 1952 | 1,386 | 330 (*23.8*) | 25 (*1.8*) | 512 (*36.9*) | 220 (*15.9*) | 299 (*21.6*) |
| 1953 | 1,529 | 372 (*24.3*) | 27 (*1.8*) | 528 (*34.5*) | 253 (*16.5*) | 349 (*22.8*) |
| 1954 | 1,728 | 435 (*25.2*) | 32 (*1.9*) | 531 (*30.7*) | 281 (*16.3*) | 448 (*25.9*) |
| 1955 | 1,876 | 467 (*24.9*) | 37 (*2.0*) | 538 (*28.7*) | 322 (*17.2*) | 512 (*27.3*) |
| 1956 | 1,944 | 477 (*24.5*) | 44 (*2.3*) | 572 (*29.4*) | 367 (*18.9*) | 484 (*24.9*) |
| 1957 | 2,035 | 525 (*25.8*) | 53 (*2.6*) | 572 (*28.1*) | 415 (*20.4*) | 469 (*23.0*) |
| 1958 | 2,075 | 529 (*25.5*) | 61 (*2.9*) | 517 (*24.9*) | 463 (*22.3*) | 505 (*24.3*) |
| 1959 | 2,539 | 685 (*29.0*) | 67 (*2.8*) | 494 (*20.9*) | 513 (*21.7*) | 600 (*25.4*) |
| 1960 | 2,537 | 732 (*28.9*) | 69 (*2.7*) | 594 (*23.4*) | 538 (*21.2*) | 603 (*23.8*) |
| 1961 | 2,478 | 754 (*30.4*) | 76 (*3.1*) | 546 (*22.0*) | 594 (*24.0*) | 508 (*20.5*) |
| 1962 | 2,405 | 758 (*31.5*) | 87 (*3.6*) | 498 (*20.7*) | 625 (*26.0*) | 438 (*18.2*) |

Because the size of the sample varies from year to year, we have to be careful, of course, in comparing, for example, the gross income for 1954 (earned by 2,892 companies) with that for 1962 (earned by 1,981 companies). But the trends shown by the figures in brackets in my table are indisputable. There is no denying, for example, that the percentage of gross income paid out in Ordinary and Preference dividends has risen steadily throughout the period (although there have been setbacks). There is equally no denying that the figures support Labour's thesis; the proportion of gross income paid out in taxation has steadily declined from a third or more to around a fifth.

But a great deal more needs to be said. On dividends, the table starts, of course, when a decade and more of controls was to come to an end. Let's not blink the issue. We were faced with the choice either of ending those controls and allowing the capitalist system to adjust

54

itself to the fact that it would never see the 1938 pound again, or of permitting the Clores of this world to take over that system for about a third of its up-to-date worth. It wasn't an easy choice, but, on grounds of common justice, who would dispute that we made the right decision?

On taxation, I would presume that a good deal of the decline in the proportion of gross income absorbed by this charge reflects our deliberate efforts to give British industry incentives to invest more heavily; certainly, the rise in the proportion of income devoted to 'depreciation and other provisions' broadly matches the decline in the taxation percentage.

I can't believe that these spokesmen of the Labour Party want to see these incentives abolished. Are they perhaps bothered, as Socialists always seem to be bothered, by the apparent impossibility of making this country prosperous without conferring some degree of prosperity on the owners of the equity of that country's industry? Does their attitude reflect the dream of so many Socialists that one day their party will succeed in creating an industrial boom which leaves the Stock Exchange out in the cold?

Let them look again at these Board of Trade figures, and they will find that even a Conservative government has come remarkably close to achieving these objectives. Cross my heart and hope to die, the figures in my table are official, true and complete. At least, they are complete as far as they go. Let's take them a little further – remembering that these are still official figures, not something cooked up by that fellow Wincott.

They are indeed a continuation of the official figures I used in a previous article, showing that whereas the profits earned by the sample of companies included in this Board of Trade analysis had apparently increased very substantially, you got a very different picture when you related the profits, gross or net, to the assets, gross or net, employed in earning them.

Whereas gross income represented 20.0 per cent of gross assets in 1950, by 1961 the percentage had fallen to 14.2 per cent; whereas net income was 21.4 per cent of net assets in the former year, by 1961 it was down to 13.8 per cent. Well, the melancholy process continued in 1962 – the gross return fell again, to 13.3 per cent, and the net to 12.7 per cent.

Now look at those dividends and interest payments which in my table appear to have increased so inordinately – by nearly 160 per cent since 1950, isn't it? Relate them to the real capital employed by these companies and what do you find? That the investor's average reward for financing a very substantial increase in assets in 1962 amounted to 4.7 per cent gross and 5.9 per cent net, compared with 4.9 per cent and 6.1 per cent respectively 12 years earlier.

Now I'm not arguing for a moment that the rates of profitability ruling in 1950 were or should be sacrosanct. I'm just suggesting that *all* the facts of capitalism in Britain in 1964 ought to be made known to the great British public. I said earlier in this article that because the size of the sample of companies covered in this Board of Trade survey varies from year to year we have to be careful in comparing the total gross income for 1954 with the total gross income for 1962.

There is no reason, however (provided we get our sums right), why we should not calculate from these figures the experience of the *average* company in various years. I have in fact done so, and a very illuminating exercise it is. The average company in 1962 had gross assets of £9,140,000, earned a gross income of £1,214,000, and paid out gross dividends and interest amounting to £426,000. The average company in 1950 employed gross assets of £2,379,000 to earn £476,000 and to pay out £117,500.

Does the great British public (and the economists of the Labour Party) think this £6¾ million extra of assets employed by the average company just grew on trees, or was produced by mirrors? Or does it acknowledge that it was largely put up, directly or indirectly, by investors? If it admits the latter, does it expect to get the use of £6¾ million extra assets from the average company for free? Would Mr Callaghan run the National Savings Movement or the State Unit Trust on which he seems so keen on the proposition that investors should get no reward for so greatly increasing the capital our economy needs?

'Of course not', I can hear our Jim saying. 'I'm the most reasonable of men'. Well, Jim, as a reasonable man, work out, will you, what the *extra* dividends and interest the average company paid out in 1962 represented as a gross return on the *extra* assets it was employing compared with 1950. You haven't got your slide rule? Don't bother. Let me oblige you. H'm. £308,500 on £6,761,000. H'm. Just over 4½ per cent, Jim.

Let me end this article by putting certain simple propositions to you all. First, we've all of us done a lot better since 1950. Our standard of living has risen by 40 per cent; the car population (Heaven help us) has more than doubled; we have something like seven TV sets for each one we had in 1950. Secondly, despite our mixed economy and despite all the shortcomings of British capitalism, it is predominantly that capitalism which has done these things. We now discover that it has done them by putting up enormous sums of new money for an overall return which Lord Mackintosh himself would admit (has indeed admitted) is not sufficient to attract a proper level of support to the National Savings Movement's investments.

Thirdly, isn't it time that British capitalism, with all the vast resources at its disposal, found a way of getting the truth about itself – the 4½ per cent truth – over to the public, instead of allowing the Wilsons, the Callaghans and the Jays of this world to get away with murder?

# The red queen and the pink chancellor

22 June 1965

IT was an American friend of mine, visiting this country recently, who suggested I should bring up to date, so far as UK and US equities at least were concerned, the exercise I published here towards the end of 1962, the object of which was to see how the Ordinary shares of various countries had performed in real terms.

I then took *The Financial Times* Industrial share index year by year since its base date (1 July 1935) and deflated it by the cost-of-living index. I did the same with the Dow Jones Industrial average, deflating that by the US Department of Labour consumer price index.

I find that, where the Dow average has this year soared in real terms to 3¼ times its 1935 worth, the FT index in similar terms is still 7 per cent below its level of thirty years ago.

Discount the figures as you will, they pose a number of pretty disturbing questions. In the light of the trends they show, are the discriminatory effects of the corporation tax against portfolio investment in the US going to have the effect the Government obviously reckons they will? Are long-term investors going to give up the substance – the enhancement in real terms of both capital and income – for the shadow, the apparently higher return (in monetary terms) to be obtained by a switch to an economy which treats its investors so shabbily?

Over the short-term, the exchange may seem to pay off. But many of these investors aren't interested in the short-term. They want to protect the substance of their investments.

Clearly, on the record, you don't do that in British equities. And that raises another devastating question, a simple 'Why not?' You may argue the FT index is not representative. Some Americans argue the same way about the Dow; they calculate, for example, where the average would be to-day had IBM not been excluded from it. As both are based on 30 shares we can at least say like is being compared with like.

In fact, both are more representative than their critics contend. The divergencies between the old FT index and the 500-share FT-Actuaries index since the latter was started in April, 1962, have been very small. The Standard and Poor index of 500 US Common stocks gives the same broad picture as the Dow.

Anyway, you can't just argue away the fact that for almost 30 years now (the FT index will be celebrating its birthday in a little over a week) 30 of Britain's biggest industrial undertakings have been ploughing back millions and millions of money, and have raised millions and millions more by new issues, to no real benefit of their shareholders; to produce a result less than a third as good as the same processes have secured for American stockholders.

You can argue, of course, that just because our performance has been so abysmally bad, the scope in our equities could be enormous, once we start to put things right. I have myself argued in this fashion. But to argue thus you have to make one fundamental premise – that we want to put things right.

In a way, I'm sure this Government wants to do so. But there is a depressing volume of evidence to demonstrate that it wants to do so without benefiting investors in the process. When I wrote my original piece on the real performance of the FT index on 20 November 1962, I said that that performance justified Mr Selwyn Lloyd's decision to restrict his tax on capital profits to short-term gains.

I pointed out that it would be a monstrous thing to tax away part of the paper profit the house purchaser of 1935 has enjoyed, and that it

## Profits and Productivity

'would be equally monstrous to impose what in fact would be a capital levy in the guise of a long-term tax on Stock Exchange capital gains when there haven't been any real capital gains'.

Well, for political purposes, the Labour Government accepts the logic of the one argument but, equally for political reasons, rejects the other. It imposes a vicious and penal capital gains tax on paper share profits. I suppose there has been no more revealing observation in the whole of the debate on the Finance Bill than Mr Niall MacDermot's justification of our 30 per cent rate for individuals.

That rate, he said, was not unreasonably relative to America's 25 per cent, because our top rate of income taxation was $91\frac{1}{4}$ per cent, whereas theirs was 70 per cent. If you can overlook the misrepresentation about the rate of America's capital gains tax (which is probably in fact about a third of ours) you are still left with the depressing argument that because a man is handicapped by having a withered leg, you may as well break one of his arms to level things up. You don't win gold medals in the economic Olympic Games when you're governed by such men.

On top of this, of course, you have the corporation tax, with its avowed intention of shifting some of the burden of taxation from the individual to the company; with its effective cut, however much profits may rise, of around a fifth in shareholders' entitlement; with its body-blows to many of our finest businesses with their overseas operations; and so on.

To pretend that such a Government is really interested in re-producing here the sense of dynamic, the rewards for thrift and striving and risk-taking which have taken the American economy and its shareholders so far during the last 30 years seems to me to be absolute poppy-cock.

In the looking-glass world of the Red Queen, it took all the running you could do to stay in the same place. Under the long-term capital gains tax of a Pink Chancellor, and on the record of the last 30 years, no matter how fast the average investor (represented by the index) runs, he will be way behind his starting point at the end of the race.

Indeed, for such an investor, Mr Callaghan's tax has the exquisite effect (from a Socialist point of view) that the greater the inflation, the worse in real terms the average investor does on realisation. If his portfolio keeps pace with the index, and there's a 20 per cent inflation, his original £100 is worth, after tax, £114 paper value and £95 real value on realisation; 50 per cent inflation gives £135 net paper and £90 real; 100 per cent inflation gives £170 net paper and £85 real.

You can put the matter another way. If you assume that the index over the long term keeps pace with inflation (and as we've seen, over the last thirty years, it hasn't) any portfolio even to maintain its value in real terms has to beat the index by 50 per cent. How many investors can hope to do that?

All unwittingly, I suspect, Mr George Brown summed it up recently by placing in juxtaposition the 'more of us (who) live by earning rather than owning', the implication clearly being that the earners are a jolly sight more important than the owners, which latter ought in the interests of the former to be clouted over the head at every possible opportunity.

In the United States, where the earners don't do so badly but where the owners aren't regarded as something the cat brought in, the gross national product has quadrupled in real terms over the period we have been examining, whereas ours, also in real terms, has only doubled. Mr Brown's formula doesn't seem to work as well as America's, even where the horny-handed sons of toil are concerned.

Perhaps someone will tell Mr Callaghan so during his forthcoming visit to Washington?

# Holborn Circus, Belgrade and all that

17 August 1965

I SEEM to recall a cartoon in *Punch*, during one of our early post-war crises, depicting an elderly retired couple sitting in deckchairs by the sea. 'Let me see', said one to the other, 'where did we spend the last balance of payments crisis? Was it Bournemouth or Brighton?'

Myself, I spend week-ends these days, in the middle of the worst external crisis we have seen since 1931, watching the Channel ferries streaming back and forth like buses, carrying the foreigners whose countries can afford holidays abroad for their citizens, and the much larger number of Britishers, whose country can't. This is progress. The choice to-day is not Bournemouth or Brighton, but Cavalaire or the Costa Brava.

# Profits and Productivity

The *Daily Mirror* is very properly worried about the apparently complete ignorance of the economic facts of life among most of the British people. So last week, on Monday, Tuesday and Wednesday, it devoted the best part of two pages each day, in the front of the book, telling its readers all about the appalling mess we're in, how we got into it, and how the *Mirror* reckons we should get out of it.

It was a blast-off, all right. 'Abrasive' is a switched-on word these days, since the *Economist* used it to describe Ted Heath. This was definitely abrasive stuff. It might have been printed on sand-paper.

The job was superlatively well done. The facts were right. The diagnosis excellent. The approach was non-partisan, politically. There was nothing about a bankers' ramp; the *Mirror* was quite kindly to the City. No reference to profits or dividends as the villain of the piece. If the 20 million – or whatever the figure is – readership of the *Mirror* doesn't know what the economic score is, that's not the *Mirror's* fault.

Mind you, some of us could have wished that when the *Mirror* published all those pictures of the worst slums it could find in Britain just before the last election, it had pointed out that even a Labour Government wouldn't get rid of them without the drastic action the *Mirror* is now advocating. But we mustn't carp.

What we may do is to consider whether both the remedies, and the *Mirror* technique, admirable as it is, will do the trick. First, the remedies.

Item I: Devaluation and a National Government alike are out.

Item II: Our spending abroad must be drastically curtailed. It's the chopper for imports, holidays abroad, military bases overseas, aid to underdeveloped countries. In particular, Mr Wilson's strange throwback to Rudyard Kipling gets kicked.

Item III: Import quotas must come on and the import surcharge go off.

Item IV: A payroll tax must be introduced to 'impose a penalty on lazy managements who hog a disproportionate share of the country's labour force'.

Item V: All indirect taxes must be raised 10 per cent.

Item VI: Internal Government expenditure must be slashed and the Government machine drastically overhauled.

Item VII: Lazy, timid management and Luddite trade unionists alike have got to disappear.

# The Business of Capitalism

Well, now, I have the best of reasons for agreeing with most of this. And the parts I don't agree with, and the bits I would like to see put in, are partially at least wrapped up with the query I raised about the *Mirror* technique.

This is, after all, a mixture of exposure and exhortation. There is nothing wrong with that – after all, it's all that any crusading newspaper can do. I certainly don't agree with Lord Erroll who, in a letter to *The Times* in which he comments on the *Mirror* articles, wants someone to take the lazy managers and the Luddite unionists on one side and read them the Riot Act, but quietly, so no one else, particularly the foreigner, can hear. The foreigners aren't that stupid. They use our docks. And London Airport.

But the *Mirror* itself admits that it exposes nothing that is new, which leaves just the exhortation. Well, some of us have been exhorting governments, managements and unions to pull their fingers out for years. The *Mirror* itself has.

I recall that last March it had an earlier go. One article asked whether we wanted to commit national suicide and urged the case for entry into the Common Market. Another, inspired I think I may say by an article I wrote, told *Mirror* readers the story of William Denby and how that company saw off a 16-month-old strike, retrained 'green' labour and finished up with greater productivity and profits 70 per cent up.

But you can't go on using sandpaper for ever. Marjorie Proops and the pictures and comic strips are much more fun. People get browned-off, I know. There's a chap up in Glasgow who wants the Stock Exchange Council to censor my articles – the ones which say that the time's not ripe for stimulating the economy, that is. So here's the *Mirror* back at it again, and the people read it and hop on the boat for Calais and go on being lazy and inefficient and obstructive when they come back.

Now the *Mirror*, for all its impartiality on the present occasion, is a paper of the Left. The true Left doesn't rely on exhortation. If some of our Communist trade unionists behaved in the home of Communism as they behave here, *Pravda* wouldn't write three articles telling them not to. They'd find themselves in a labour camp, pdq.

We don't do things like that. But we could still learn from the Communists, stop exhorting people to be good and yet preserve our democratic habits.

# Profits and Productivity

I don't think the chaps who wrote the articles in the *Mirror* can have seen a piece the East European Correspondent of the FT wrote in the issue of 3 August. This is a pity, for if they had, there could have been an Item VIII, which would have made some at least of the other items quite unnecessary.

Yugoslavia, it seems, is not so very different from Britain. She has been suffering from 'wild inflation, balance of payments deficit, sluggish productivity in her factories'. Because of this, the dinar has been devalued. (We don't need to do that, as the Mirror says.) But the Yugoslav Government 'is now trying to give a hard, competitive tone to the economy in order to restore it to health' (which, of course, is just what the *Mirror* – and some others – want to happen here).

Maybe the Yugoslav papers wrote fine, exhortatory articles. But the Government did something else. It cut all tariffs in half, 'in the hope . . . that foreign goods will offer a steady competition to domestic products and so prevent further inflationary price increases'.

Of course, factories will now have an incentive to export more, but prices of raw materials, fuel and food, which have been held down, will rise, thus squeezing manufacturers between higher costs and more competitive prices. 'Some factories may find it difficult to survive at all', the FT man said. It seems the Government isn't over anxious that they should. Some of them are in what we would call 'development areas', and local political lobbies are expected to get busy. But all over Yugoslavia, people are going to find their real incomes reduced.

Looking further ahead, however, the Government expects 'consolidation and perhaps genuine progress in production and productivity'. I hope the FT man will keep us informed of the progress of this Communist experiment in the economics of Adam Smith. It ought to be jolly interesting.

By the way, a little bird tells me that Mr Cecil King got Mr Hugh ('Publish and be Damned') Cudlipp back from West Africa to take command of these *Mirror* articles. It seems a pity he didn't come home via Belgrade.

# How to counteract the spotty ones

31 August 1965

FRANKLY, I thought it rated higher as a tuck-in than a teach-in. The occasion? A small gathering, round the dinner table, of a leading industrialist, some bods who are concerned with keeping bright and burnished the image free enterprise, private enterprise, capitalism, or whatever you like to call it, and five cynical, hard-boiled, disillusioned and ageing financial journalists.

The subject? The best way of expressing a shareholder's return on capital. I got it all wrong at the beginning. I thought we were going to talk about earnings on real capital employed, how to define them, how to make them rise, whether all companies should be compelled to print a record of them for the last ten years on the first page of the annual report – in red ink.

But no. The object of the exercise was to see if there is some way of preventing the use (or rather, the misuse) of the percentages for dividends and earnings related to nominal capital which so mislead the uninformed, and provide such splendid ammunition for the Socialists. This discovery depressed me, for two reasons.

First, believe it or not, I wrote my first article advocating no par value shares 25 years ago come next May. And it's 15 years, almost to the day, since I wrote an article here 'Why Not Abolish the Percentage Sign?', in which I put forward exactly the same arguments that I heard as we ate that very excellent meal. I did say the financial journalists were cynical, hard-boiled, disillusioned and ageing, didn't I?

The second reason for my depression is much more important. In what passes for the capitalist world in Britain to-day, the merits or demerits of the percentage sign have become, relatively, supremely unimportant. Even the TUC, which in its evidence to the Gedge Committee on no par value shares in 1953 'strongly opposed' NPV because of the 'suspicion' such shares would create among workpeople, had dropped its opposition to them by the time the Jenkins Committee on company law amendment sat in the early sixties. That same Jenkins Committee did recommend NPV shares, which would, of course, cause percentages to disappear.

No, what we ought to have discussed at that dinner, what everybody concerned with capitalism ought to be discussing, is the sug-

64

gestion, inherent in the contention that ploughed back profits aren't capital subscribed by shareholders and don't belong to them, that all Ordinary shareholders are entitled to *is* a percentage dividend – a fixed percentage dividend at that.

You may think I'm being alarmist, but I'm not. Mr Callaghan's corporation tax, which effectively separates shareholders from their companies and discourages equity issues, is in fact the blown-up successor to Neville Chamberlain's 5 per cent National Defence Contribution introduced nearly 30 years ago. Mr Chamberlain, as you may remember, was a High Tory.

It's a way we have in Britain, and it needs watching. There's at least one member of the present Government who has argued for years that company reserves don't belong to shareholders, but to the community, to the workpeople and the consumer; he wrote a booklet about it, for the Fabian Society.

Another Labour M.P., who took part in a filibuster in 1952 on a Tory M.P.'s private Bill to make NPV shares permissive, said that for every £1 of profits ploughed back into a business, a company should be compelled to issue one pound's worth of debentures, to be held by the Government, 'so that the community could get at any rate some return on what customers had been overcharged'.

So don't say it couldn't happen here. There was enough evidence in the correspondence that followed my piece in *The Financial Times* on 20 July ('Taking the Equity out of Equities') to demonstrate that it could; that the leopards don't change their spots. For myself, I don't expect them to. Being a liberal-minded cove, I don't even dislike them for being spotty. They probably think I'm striped.

But I would like to see a much better job done to counteract the insidious propaganda of the spotty ones. I would like it to be made plain to every holder of a with-profit life policy, to every contributor to a company pension scheme, to every vicar and curate whose increased stipends spring from the Church Commissioners' decision in 1948 to buy equities, to every widow the Public Trustee looks after, to every unit-trust investor and investment club member, what the result would have been over the last 20 years if these Socialist ideas had been implemented.

How, in fact, they would have fared had their equities ranked with Hugh Dalton's 2½ per cent Treasuries (issued at 100, present price 38;

purchasing power of the interest, in real terms, now less than half of
what it was in 1946). My chart gives you the picture.

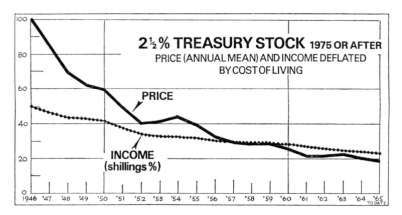

In short, I agree with the Salvationists; I don't see why the Devil
should have all the good tunes.

But that's not enough. Mr R. J. Fletcher, a fellow co-operator of
mine, was one of the spotty ones who wrote to the Editor of *The
Financial Times* (three letters) following my article. Mr Fletcher was
arguing the case for emasculated equities. He gave examples of four
carefully selected shares which, over a carefully selected period, had
done fabulously well.

He was arguing, of course, that it would have been more equitable
if the bulk of this fabulous appreciation had accrued to the companies'
workers and consumers. What he didn't mention was that one of his
whizz-stocks, City Centre Properties, has fallen back from its 1960
high of 73s 3d to 23s 7½d to-day, which makes his argument that the
element of risk-taking in equities is negligible seem a little odd.
Would the workers and tenants of City Centre as of 1960 think it more
equitable if they shared in that 67½ per cent depreciation? 

Another Mr Fletcher mentioned was Jaguar, where the shares over
the last two years have fallen by a mere 45 per cent. However, they're
still well up on the 1950 price, and Mr Fletcher doubtless still argues
it would have been more equitable if the bulk of the net appreciation
had accrued to Jaguar workers and consumers.

Well, why didn't it? It's a free country, and Jaguar are a free
market (at least, the 'A' shares are). On Mr Fletcher's own evidence,

66

all every Jaguar worker and consumer needed in 1950 to share in this bonanza was a hundred pounds, which in the Affluent Society isn't much (two weeks on the Costa Brava?) Jaguar workers aren't among the lowest paid, and Jaguar consumers, by definition, shouldn't be pushed for £100.

But even good tunes and wider share-ownership aren't enough. They represent one fist of the two-fisted attack I long to see. The other fist would carry a bolo punch for the nastiness of capitalism.

For the secret scheme under which a handful of chaps can make a fortune without the people who put up most of the money having a clue as to what was going on; for the very private arrangements under which a chairman could have drawn £270,000 a year, and the more the company borrowed the more he drew; for the insiders who abuse their fiduciary positions by buying and selling shares on confidential information.

I know such nastinesses are the exception and not the rule. I know we have encouraged them by our taxation system. But they shouldn't happen; they do great damage to our cause; they are an absolute gift to the spotty ones. We can only pray that one of these days we shall get a government with the courage to see that they don't happen – and that the right things, the positive things, do.

Like having a taxation system which puts nastinesses at a discount; like providing honest, decent incentives; like not humbugging about the need to save and then discriminating against the fruit of saving, by calling it unearned income.

You know, all the square, unfashionable things, that backward countries like the United States do.

# Barking up the wrong trees

## 7 September 1965

IT might, I thought, be something of a service, amidst all the activities of the politicians, Sir Maurice Laing, Messrs Aubrey Jones, George Woodcock, John Davies, *et al*, if we sat back and had a look at some figures.

The source for my figures is the invaluable statistical section of the reviews of the National Institute of Economic and Social Research, the latest of which reviews, you may recall, was not exactly joyful about our longer-term economic prospects.

I have taken what seem to me to be apposite statistics for the UK and four other leading countries: the USA, West Germany, France and Japan. I am as sceptical as the next man as to the exact reliance we can put on these international comparisons. But, on the whole, the broad picture they portray makes sense.

But it is not, very often, the picture as popularly drawn. Mr Brown, I read, has been telling the TUC that Britain faces bankruptcy unless inflation is brought to a halt. Certainly we must stop inflation, but it doesn't seem that the rise in our cost of living has got out of hand relative to other people's.

The US, of course, is famed for the relative stability of its price structure these days. But it's a bit surprising to find that our prices have been running virtually level with Germany's now for nearly eight years. And compared with France and Japan, we seem to have been the soul of moderation.

Well, then, what about wages? Didn't we learn only last week that the chaps working in our manufacturing industries are now knocking up on average nearly a thousand a year? Take a look at the figures showing what has happened to hourly earnings in the manufacturing industries of the five countries. There's nothing very horrific about our increases in earnings relative to those secured in Japan, Western Germany or France. It is, indeed, only American workers who have enjoyed a more modest increase than ours, and they, of course, started from a very much higher level than anyone else.

If we deflate the indices of hourly earnings by those of consumer prices, to give a rough measure of real earnings, we find that West German workers have done best (151), the Japanese come second (133), the British third (128), the French fourth (124) and the Americans last (115). Not altogether what everyone would have expected, but once more, nothing disastrous about the British position.

If we turn next to wage costs per unit of output, there's nothing very much for us to keen about there, either. America once again heads this league, with Germany and France (in recent years) falling to the bottom places, and ourselves and the Japanese in the middle of the table.

Doesn't all this suggest that we may, in the current frenzy of activity over the Government's prices and incomes policy at least be putting the emphasis in the wrong places, if indeed we're not barking up the wrong trees altogether? And when you look at the figures for export prices of manufacturers and output per manhour worked in manufacturing industries these suspicions stand strengthened.

The figures showing output per manhour worked are the crucial ones. Here, at the latest date for which the NIESR tables give common figures, we were clearly holding the wooden spoon. Japan and Western Germany have roared ahead, and France and the US come third and fourth.

There is some indication that we have been doing better in the first part of 1965 and Western Germany a little worse. But there is little doubt that it is on these figures that all the gentlemen I mentioned at the beginning of this article should be concentrating their attention.

It seems a fair deduction, too, that these lead inevitably to the figures for export prices of manufactures. Once more, these are not as catastrophic from our point of view as we are sometimes led to believe. But there is not much for our comfort in them.

American export prices have, of course, benefited from the general, remarkable stability in prices and wage costs in recent years. France clearly must be a special case, with the benefits to exports of the 1958 devaluation showing up in the early part of the period we are looking at and the disadvantages appearing more recently, with consumer prices and wage costs per unit of output shooting ahead.

The really outstanding performance is Japan's, where despite the biggest rise in internal prices and in hourly earnings, export prices have fallen almost continuously. We have done slightly worse than Western Germany (and of course a good deal worse than our other competitors). But there seems little doubt that if our output per manhour worked had risen as strongly as it has in, say, Western Germany and Japan, our exports would have been more competitive than those of our main rivals, and their availability very much improved.

The more you brood over these figures, the more you are forced to conclude that our economic doctors are making a faulty diagnosis. The symptoms of the English Disease, as it is now known the world over, are not excessive rises in incomes and prices, period. Most other countries have these symptoms to an even more marked degree than we have.

The real cause of the English Disease is poor productivity. If only the TUC at this week's meetings – and, of course, the Confederation of British Industry – would learn the lesson that shrieks aloud from the figures, our troubles would be over. That lesson is, quite simply, that the three countries where hourly earnings have risen most – Japan, Western Germany and France – are the three countries where output per manhour has risen most.

Of course, you will say, we knew this already. Why, then, is all this tremendous emphasis being placed on the quite negative and inherently damaging prices and incomes policy? To impress the foreigners? I doubt whether they are as naive as that. They know the real cause of the English Disease.

They know that all the efforts of Mr George Brown, indeed all those of Mr Aubrey Jones, are the efforts of well-intentioned men. But they know they are really only gimmicks compared with the real problems which sooner or later will have to be overcome. It is like using a tack-hammer to break boulders – the boulders of restrictive practices, misuse of manpower and age-old attitudes of mind which account for our poor showing on productivity.

There must be, there are, more direct, forthright and expeditious ways of breaking these boulders. They will not be popular among trade unionists or industrialists. But it is Government's job to find them and use them.

# On turning $2 million into $86 million

15 February 1966

THE ghosts of the 1965 Finance Act refuse to lie down. A few weeks back, Professor E. E. Hagen, Professor of Economics and Political Science at the Massachusetts Institute of Technology, wrote a letter to the Editor of the *Economist* pointing out that our *trade* deficit was no larger in the 'sixties than it had been in the 'fifties.

In the three years 1953–55 it averaged £254 million; in the three years 1962–64, it averaged £237 million. But whereas in the first period government expenditures abroad on current account totalled £695 million, in the second they almost doubled at £1,304 million.

## Profits and Productivity

Samuel Brittan presented much the same picture in his article in the Pink 'Un on 7 February, 'Do We Spend Too Much Abroad?' Lord Cromer rubbed it in his speech to the Overseas Bankers Club the same evening.

It would be too much to ask us to believe that these three gentlemen (and others even earlier, said he modestly) were engaged in a conspiracy. The plain fact cannot be gainsaid. If government expenditure overseas had been held down, there would have been no balance of payments crisis in 1964–65, and we should have been spared much of the misery of the last sixteen months.

This was not the picture presented to the British public, however. Assiduously the idea was propagated that it was excessive investment overseas which was our undoing. And this, of course, was one of the justifications, if not *the* justification for last year's fiscal revolution.

But the accusation against investment went deeper than that. 'We have allowed overseas investment', said Mr Callaghan in the budget debate, 'not so much on the direct side and not so much in relation to trade and commerce, but especially in relation to portfolio investment – securities – to grow almost uncontrolled through the medium of the investment currency market'. Hence the corporation tax. Hence the expropriation of 25 per cent of the dollar premium whenever an overseas stock is sold, which puts skilled management at such a disadvantage. Hence, the recent new tax treaty with the United States.

Mr Callaghan's statement in fact is completely unsubstantiated by the official figures. In 1960, portfolio investors overall brought home £37 million, in 1961, £28 million and in 1962, £39 million. True, in 1963, they added £14 million to their overseas holdings and in 1964, £7 million. But is an investment of £7 million in one year, of £21 million in two years, a disinvestment of £83 million over a five-year period, 'uncontrolled growth'?

Lord Cromer's was a magnificent speech which, alas, got very little publicity, because, ironically enough, the stiffer hire-purchase controls necessitated by excessive Government spending overseas and not by uncontrolled portfolio investment occupied all the front pages on Tuesday.

I would like to quote and discuss one or two of his remarks. Here, he said, in effect, is one field of special skills and expertise where we have held on to and even increased the lead we had, say, a century ago.

# The Business of Capitalism

'It is interesting', said Lord Cromer, 'to compare the performance of funds which have had the benefit of professional management and freedom to go in and out of the market at judgment with those which for some reason or another have not had the same freedom. The difference in result can be very striking. The balance of payments has certainly benefited from the skill that exists in this field in this country and north of the border'.

We don't need to theorise about this; the evidence supplied by the Alliance Trust and set out in my table speaks for itself. The Alliance Trust lost virtually all its dollar assets during the last war; since 1948, in this Dundee parable of the talents, $2 million has been turned into $86 million.

## HOW ALLIANCE TRUST DID IT

| Periods to January 31 | Dollars acquired during the preceding five years ($m.) | Accumulated total of dollars acquired ($m.) | Market value of investments held ($m.) | Income of the preceding year ($m.) | Yield on dollars acquired % |
|---|---|---|---|---|---|
| 1953 | 9.9 | *11.9 | 15.7 | 0.7 | 5.9 |
| 1958 | 8.3 | 20.2 | 33.0 | 1.4 | 6.9 |
| 1963 | 4.8 | 25.0 | 66.1 | 1.9 | 7.6 |
| 1965 (2 years) | 1.5 | 26.5 | 86.1 | 2.5 | 9.5 |

(* Includes securities held at 31 January 1948, valued at $2m.)

The Alliance Trust is not unique, of course. Taking out the effect of the $10 million loan raised in the US in 1963, the British Assets Trust multiplied $2.1 million in 1948 to $46.4 million by last September, and was earning over 12 per cent on the dollars acquired. There must be dozens of other, comparable cases.

How has this been done? 'We are investors seeking income, preferably growing income', said Mr Alan Brown at the last Alliance Trust meeting. 'We change our investments only to that end. We are not security traders and do not seek short term capital gains. Our business is to *invest* – long-term'.

It has been done at no cost to the country's official gold and exchange reserves (although, as the ambivalent Mr Wilson told the New York bankers, it has certainly buttressed our overall reserves marvellously). It has been done almost entirely through the investment dollar pool, paying the premium which, of course, reflects the state of supply and demand and not the value of our currency.

It has been done, ironically enough, because the Labour Government in 1947 had the good sense to pass an Exchange Control Act which permitted it, and negotiated tax treaties which undeniably gave an incentive to portfolio investment overseas. It has been done in modest offices, with modest Boards and modest managements. I doubt whether they've got a computer among them. True, one or two chaps from each group do visit the US and Canada regularly, but never were dollars better spent.

Why is it then that such a harmless and beneficial process arouses so much hostility and animosity? It is not just the present Labour Government which seems to hate it. Ted Heath was behind Jim Callaghan in the debate I have already quoted. He seemed to think there was some diggy-poggy going on in 'the switch market' and pledged his support for anything Jim did to stop it.

First, then, it seems to be sheer ignorance that is responsible, and here what we call 'the City' must be to blame. Secondly, there is the instinctive feeling that you have to have a massive industrial complex, employing a highly expensive chairman, dozens of multilingual salesmen giving themselves ulcers chasing orders all over the world in planes, dirty great computers, tens of thousands of horny-handed sons of toil working in factories, millions and millions of pounds of imported raw materials, before you are really 'worthwhile'.

We've had the same attitude for years towards our overseas debtors who don't pay up. We'd rather give them fresh credit for unrequited exports, because that looks good in the trade returns, and makes employment in an already nominally over-fully employed country even fuller, than make them pay up for goods we 'sold' them decades ago.

We just don't like the little man who sits in a dingy office in a back street and buys and sells commodities we've never heard of and which may never enter this country but whose operations earn him profits and benefit our bank, insurance and shipping companies too.

Here, what I believe to be one of our cardinal sins, envy, enters into it. If we *were* willing to admit that our investment trusts do a good job for the country, which obviously some of us aren't, we can't stomach the fact that they do a good job for their 'functionless excrescences' in the process.

73

We're inhibited about making our debtors pay up, because some speculator in 'busted bonds' may double his money. We don't like the little man in the dingy office in the back street because he makes a jolly sight more than we do without ever getting up off his bottom.

I can only say it's all very sad. And a bit worrying. Whatever the rest of us are or do, the leaders of the nation ought not to distort or misrepresent figures simply to justify age-old prejudices or ignorance. And we ought to remember that chap Hagen I mentioned in my opening paragraph.

Foreigners aren't as stupid or as prejudiced as we seem to be. They study the figures, and draw the right conclusions. They see us giving priority not to the investments which literally saved our lives in two world wars but to a string of overseas bases which in due course become derelict and abandoned and which won't be worth a cent if we ever face another life and death struggle. They see how we deliberately set out to cripple people who can turn $2 million into $86 million in less than 20 years. They must think we're stark, staring mad.

# 4

# Investment and Finance

# The vicar's shares

9 February 1960

IN Bedfordshire, there lives a vicar who is also an investor. Talking about investment, he'll agree with you that *technically* (his italics) the shares he receives as the result of a capitalisation issue are not 'free'. But in *practice* (his italics) these shares do 'mean extra money for nothing'.

Even more to the point, he'll demonstrate to you conclusively what he means from his own experience. Why, didn't he get 200 'bonus' shares from Barclays Bank not so long ago? Of course the price for the shares fell when the new ones were issued. But bless your soul, it soon recovered, and to-day it's higher than it was before the capitalisation issue was announced. And this isn't at all unusual. The vicar can quote you dozens of similar cases. Doesn't that prove his point?

Bless *his* soul, the vicar's a good chap. A scrip issue's a boon to his youth club; it means the club can have that new equipment it needs so badly. And the next one will mean a new car for the vicar without bothering the PCC for help. A real Aladdin's Lamp, these 'bonus' issues.

With the vicar in mind – and I assure you I'm not kidding you about him – I've been looking at those excessively dull and complicated documents, allotment letters, with a new eye in recent months. Some of them, of course, are better than others; more concise, plainer English, less gibberish.

But as I've read and re-read the best of them, I've asked myself: 'If I were an elderly spinster in Kidderminster, or a farmer in Fife, would I really know what on earth this is all about?' And the answer must surely be a resounding 'No'.

Oh yes, I know there's that bit at the top telling you that this is a valuable document, and that if you don't understand it you should consult your stockbroker or banker or solicitor. But even assuming that your spinster in Kidderminster knows or can get to a stockbroker, banker or solicitor, what with her arthritis being what it is at this time of the year, is it really the right approach in this day and age for an enlightened company just to stuff an unintelligible document into an envelope and put the onus for finding out what it means on the shareholder?

Would it be asking too much of companies, in the interests of good

Investment and Finance

shareholder relationships, and in an attempt to warn shareholders against the trap of consuming capital in the belief that they'll be no worse off as a result, to send a covering letter on the following lines?

'DEAR SHAREHOLDER, The recent meeting of shareholders unanimously approved the proposals for the capitalisation of reserves and for the issue of new Ordinary shares on the lines foreshadowed by the directors recently.

'These new shares have now been issued in the ratio of one new share for each two held, and the enclosed formal letter of allotment shows the number of new shares which have been allotted to you.

'You are not required to make any payment for these shares. In fact, shareholders have already paid for them over the years. When each year shareholders approve dividends on the Ordinary capital which absorb less than the profits available for distribution, shareholders are in effect putting new capital into the business.

'In the company's balance-sheet the new capital represented by this ploughing back of profits, as the process is called, is reflected in a growth of assets, and, on the liabilities side, in an increase in the company's reserves. The amount of nominal capital involved in the present issue of Ordinary shares will in the next accounts be transferred from these reserves to the item "Issued Ordinary Capital".

'Your directors would like to explain, for the benefit of those shareholders who are not completely familiar with such an issue, that the fact that these shares are now being issued does not necessarily mean that the amount paid out in Ordinary dividends to shareholders will be increased. Your company, as this letter has explained, has already had the use of the money these shares represent, and the extra profits earned on it have already been reflected in the profit and loss accounts of past years.

'If your directors should, at the end of the present financial year, decide to recommend the distribution of the same amount in dividends before income-tax as last year on the capital as increased by the present issue, then the rate of the percentage dividend and the amount per share would be reduced proportionately. Last year's total dividend, you will recall, was 1s 6d a share, or 15 per cent. In the circumstances just outlined, this, as a result of the present share issue, would be reduced to 1s a share, or 10 per cent.

'This would mean, if you retained the shares now allotted to you, that your dividend income on your shareholding in this company

77

would be maintained. You are of course at liberty to sell all or part of the shares now allotted to you, just as you have been free at any time in the past to sell all or part of your shareholding before this issue was made, and provision is made in the enclosed letter of allotment for you to renounce all or some of the new shares in favour of other people.

'I would, however, like to make two points to you should you dispose of all or some of the shares now allotted to you. First, the proceeds of the sale would be capital. Secondly, you should appreciate that your proportionate stake in the company would be reduced, and, in the event of the directors not increasing the amount distributed by the company as Ordinary dividend, your dividend income from this company would be smaller than it would otherwise have been. Even if and when the directors should increase the amount paid out in dividend, your dividend income from your shareholding in this company would be smaller than it would otherwise have been should you renounce all or some of these new shares.

'In fact, the primary objective of a capitalisation issue, as the present issue is called, is to bring the company's issued nominal capital into better relationship with the real capital employed in the business. Of itself, the present issue can do nothing to improve your company's earning power and hence its ability to pay higher dividends'.

Kid stuff? To you readers of *The Financial Times*, maybe. But don't forget that the Vicar is a university graduate and a highly intelligent chap. Don't forget that a former Chancellor of the Exchequer, author of a classic on *public* finance, knew so little about *private* finance that he once called these capitalisation issues 'money for jam', and clapped a prohibitive tax on them. Don't forget that a lot of people are becoming shareholders who are neither university graduates nor ex-Chancellors of the Exchequer.

Don't forget that the Government made regulations to prohibit unit trusts from distributing capital as income. Is it unduly Mrs Grundyish to see that the new investor, holding shares directly in his own right, should at least have the facts of capitalism made plain to him?

By the way, I claim no copyright in, nor perfection for, the wording of my suggested letter to shareholders. Alter it as you will; it's a good exercise putting these things in plain English, anyway. Of one thing I'm sure – any company which adopts this suggestion will be surprised at the number of grateful shareholders it will have.

# The speculator

21 June 1960

THIS week I'm really going to let my hair down, bare my soul, show you the scars of my operation, or whatever you may regard as the ultimate in revelation. For these shattering disclosures, you can thank no less a person than Mr Hugh Gaitskell, leader of HM Opposition, who spoke out on Saturday against the 'major scandal' of 'rocketing land prices'.

Land in Surrey, said Mr Gaitskell, which in 1952 fetched £1,500 an acre, now realised £8,000 an acre. A small estate in Camberley which sold in 1958 for £25,000 was resold recently in the same condition for £210,000. Speculators, property companies and land owners had benefited and had made enormous profits.

'What have these people contributed to the public good in return?' asked Mr Gaitskell, clearly knowing how the question *should* be answered. 'Precisely nothing. They have created nothing, invented nothing, organised nothing'. It was a shocking comment on Tory freedom. Mr Gaitskell believed that both equity and the need for good planning now required the extension of public ownership over the freeholds of urban land, developed or undeveloped.

Some weeks, I suspect, you think I don't know what I'm writing about in these articles. Some weeks, you may be right. But not this week. Oh dear, no. You see, I'm in the business. True, I'm not in the Charles Clore or Jack Cotton class. But just about eight years ago, I bought a piece of land, and in Surrey of all places. True, there was a house on part of it, but there's quite a substantial chunk which is rather pleasant woodland, and which, as the estate agents say, is 'ripe for development'.

Indeed, a couple of months ago, I received an unsolicited letter from a firm of estate agents telling me that land in the district was in great demand, and that if I wanted to sell please to get in touch with them. The strange thing is – and since financial journalists are supposed to be able to foretell the future, I shouldn't really be letting you in on this – eight years ago we nearly didn't buy the house because so much land went with it. 'There's an awful lot of work in the garden, dear. And just look at that frontage (it's a private road) and all those fences'.

However, there it is. If what Mr Gaitskell says is true, our spare

## The Business of Capitalism

land is worth more to-day than the house in which we live. And I'm a scandalous fellow, undeniably a landowner and speculator – if not a property company – who has contributed nothing, invented nothing, and organised nothing; and a shocking commentary on Tory freedom to boot. Bless my soul, how badly I feel about the whole business.

Me, I'd thought rather differently about it hitherto, which just shows what an ignorant clot I am. I'd thought I'd performed quite a useful function eight years ago when I'd enabled the previous owner, whose family had grown up, to move to a smaller house. You know, the most economic utilisation of the nation's resources. I thought I'd behaved rather selfishly in having three or four times as much land as I really need. Indeed, here I am writing this very article, in the wood, under the shade of a copper beech tree, whereas the land which really goes with the house is sweltering under a blazing sun.

Here we Wincotts are (I'd thought) 20 miles from London yet enjoying our seclusion, the youngest keeping her pet rabbit well away from the house, Mother enjoying the nuthatches who nest in the wood, Bill the bull terrier chasing the squirrels, the boys playing cricket on the lawn when really, I thought, we ought to sell the spare land and let two or possibly three other families share these very pleasant surroundings. But if I'd behaved unselfishly, if I'd increased the supply of building land, kept prices down or even reduced them, would Mr Gaitskell have thanked me? Not on your nelly. I'd have been a good-for-nothing, parasitical speculator, snatching his enormous profit.

My goodness, I could go on moralising about this for ages. This business about the spare land possibly being worth more than the house. That's all wrong, isn't it? Is it? You should hear my managing director on the subject when the phone rings in the study and she's in the kitchen. Or when one of the boys has measles on the top floor and there's three flights of stairs up which to carry a tray. Sometimes we stand in the wood, the two of us, and plan the contemporary, single-floor house we're going to build there when the kids have grown up. It'd be cheap at twice the price of the old one, we sometimes think. Odd, isn't it?

This business about the rise in site values being a shocking comment on Tory freedom. Chums, you ask the young married couples which they'd rather have – Socialist planning, which meant two rooms mucking in with Mum (and sharing the kitchen!) or Tory freedom, which has meant a house of their own, even if paying an economic price for what are undoubtedly very scarce resources does involve what seems to be a lot of money.

If Mr Gaitskell, the economist, really wants to observe land scarcity values as an economic phenomenon, I commend to him the study of the suburb called Toorak, in Melbourne. Australia, indubitably, has all the land in the world. But not where the citizens of Melbourne want it. We think houses and site values are expensive in Britain. They'll pay £A30,000 for a four-bedroom house, with a postage stamp garden, in Toorak, and think themselves lucky to get it.

This whole question of land values, in fact, seems to me to be just another example of the way in which we kid ourselves we can both have our cake and eat it. There are only a strictly limited number of things we can do about it. We could, as the National Federation of Building Trades Employers suggests, look into the existing density standards and green belt provisions; in other words, we could increase the supply of land. We could go in for more flat development, as they do on the Continent; in other words, we could make more economic use of the land we've got. We could carry on as we are, allowing the rise in land prices both to increase the supply and cut down the demand. About the one idea which wouldn't work is Mr Gaitskell's public ownership, which would neither increase the supply nor reduce the demand. I don't want to sell my spare land, as things are. As Mr Gaitskell would have them be, I never would.

# 'Please what is deflation?'

9 October 1962

---

*"Deflation Danger"*—*Mr. Per Jacobsson.* Headline in *The Financial Times,* September 13, 1962.

---

W HILE I was on holiday this year, I got talking with a young man. He is 33, which means he was born in 1929, left school in the late forties, graduated from university in the early fifties. The age, and these dates, are important. 'I know what inflation is', he said to me, 'but I wish someone would tell me what deflation is'.

Being some 25 years older than the young man, I reckon I'm a bit of an expert on deflation. So when I started sorting out my thoughts on the subject, I didn't expect to find many surprises. I must confess, however, that when I rummaged through the file marked 'Cost of Living', and found therein a Treasury memorandum explaining how the Civil Service does its sums when some MP asks how the present purchasing power of the £ compares with what it was once upon a time, even I got a shock.

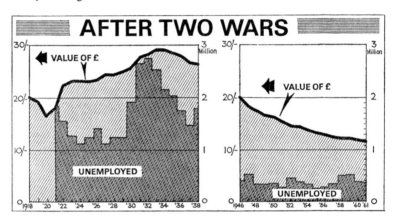

For there, on the last page of the memorandum, was a complete record of changes in the purchasing power of the £ from 1914 onwards, with the exception of the Second World War period. The results are set out in my graph. In the inter-war years, taking 1918 as a base (simply because that was the year the Kaiser's war ended) we find that the short post-war inflationary burst clipped 3s 6d off the value of the pound. Thereafter, incredible though it may seem, the real value of our currency steadily appreciated until by the middle thirties it had risen by almost 50 per cent. Even by 1938, by which time rearmament was beginning to push prices up, it was worth 26s 5d compared with 20s in 1918.

Let me tell the young man about some of the things this involved. It meant that if you got a safe job, with a bank or an insurance company, for example, you could reckon to reach a salary on which you could marry (say £350 a year or so) at around 30. Thereafter, if you were an ordinary Joe, that was more or less that. The bright chaps, of course, did better, taking on special responsibilities. The run of the mill people, however, had pretty well reached a plateau on which they would stick until they retired on pension 30 years later. (Pensions were much rarer and, of course, more precious then.)

The current concept of the regular automatic all-round hike in wages just didn't exist. But if you'd got on to the plateau in the early '20s, the real value of your £300 had become nearly £450 by 1933, so you weren't doing too badly. You were doing a jolly sight better than most other people. I'm not referring now to the millions who had no work at all. In the really bad years of the early thirties, the rise in the real value of salaries was quite often negatived by *reductions* in the monetary amounts of those salaries. I know. We had some.

What else did it mean? It meant – and this will make you laugh – that mere idle cash was not a bad growth stock. It meant that the rentier not only got his agreed, fixed rate of interest but a regular increment of something between 2 and 3 per cent per annum on top of that: the rise in the market price of $2\frac{1}{2}$ per cent. Consols from $43\frac{5}{8}$ in 1920 to $94\frac{3}{8}$ in 1935 proved how much this enhancement of income was worth in capital values. Dammit, it was pretty much like the calculations people make to-day to prove the case for Tescos.

Contrariwise, it meant that if you were in debt you had three courses open to you. You could grin and bear it. You could scrimp and save to get out of debt as soon as you could. A house mortgage, for example, was something to be repaid as soon as possible, not something to spread out for as long a period as the building society would wear. Or you could default. If you were a farmer in New South Wales or Alberta, for example, you found in effect that you had borrowed one bag of wheat, but by the time the debt matured you owed two bags. It really wasn't very surprising in the circumstances that even Commonwealth provincial governments either defaulted, or were within an inch of defaulting, on their obligations.

It meant – and explained – a very different attitude towards hire purchase. If the odds were that the goods you had your eye on would be cheaper two, three or five years later, the case for saving in advance was stronger than the case for saving retrospectively (which after all is what HP amounts to). If people then waited as long to marry as Jacob and Rachel did there were very hard economic reasons for their patience.

I could go on for a long time giving the young man further examples of 'what deflation is'. But perhaps I've said enough to give him and his contemporaries *some* idea of what it involved. You mustn't conclude from any of this that I'm arguing that our experiences of the twenties and thirties were enjoyable. For some people, of course, they were; it's a blinding glimpse of the obvious, but a rise of 50 per cent in the purchasing power of money is very beneficial to the people with money. Even for the country as a whole, these years had some surprising glimpses of better things. Did you realise that in every year save one between the early 'twenties and the late 'thirties the number of people at work in Britain *rose?*

Overall, however, no sensible person would wish to see the conditions of the 'twenties and 'thirties return. The lowest annual average for unemployment was 1,111,800 in 1927; the highest was 2,744,800 in 1932. We are still paying for that performance now. But for its (even more serious) counterpart in Germany, Hitler might have stuck to housepainting. I've always thought it was an extraordinary commentary on that period that we could – and did – regard 1936 and 1937 as boom years – with unemployment averaging 1,755,000 and 1,484,400 respectively. (In case you've forgotten, the latest count this year, on a much larger sample, was 465,000.)

What's the point, then, of recalling all this? Partly to suggest that there ought to be a happy mean between a £ which appreciates to 29s and one which depreciates to 11s 7d, which is what's happened since 1946. Partly to suggest that we keep a sense of proportion. Partly to suggest that there's a danger inherent in all this of faulty diagnosis. We are constantly getting almost hysterical pleas for pump-priming and expansion on the grand scale, because of the danger that we shall go spiralling off into a deflationary era, a world slump, or what have you. Per Jacobsson, who is no inflationist, suggested in his recent speech to the Advertising Club of Washington that financial policies should now attempt to prevent continued raw material price declines 'of a deflationary character'.

Mr Jacobsson isn't alone in this. There was a debate in the House of Lords last July in which one speaker said: 'If you take the trouble to look at the movement in agricultural prices and commodity prices in the years preceding the last great slump of 1929–30 and that of the present time, it is significant to see what a disturbing similarity there is in many of these figures. . . . Only a few months ago did the actual index of commodity prices and manufactured goods prices cross, *just as they did in 1928, a year before the great slump hit us'*. (My italics).

Now I don't deny the world is moving into an uncomfortable period. This is inevitable after most of the shortages and damage caused by the war have been made good. It's also understandable – and good – that people who lived through the years of real depression and deflation should be determined that those conditions don't return. It doesn't really make sense, however, to equate 1962 with 1928 just like that. One glance at my chart should convince you of that.

We ought, for example, to realise that one of the main reasons for the continued fall in commodity prices has been not a world slump but simply the fact that the scientist is busily engaged to-day in producing synthetic substitutes for many raw materials which 30 or 40 years ago came almost entirely from the primary producing countries. It doesn't follow that the massive creation of credit in the economies of the advanced industrial countries, which some people advocate, would touch this problem at all: if you doubled incomes here people would still buy plastic, not galvanized zinc buckets. The solution indeed may lie in quite different directions – in, for example, a much greater willingness among the advanced countries to accept the manufactured products of the developing areas, and an ending of high-cost, uneconomic production of raw materials in the advanced countries themselves.

Well, there we are. I don't know whether I've succeeded in explaining to my friend 'what deflation is'. What I do know is that if this is a deflationary world in which we're living – or even entering – I'm Zsa Zsa Gabor.

# Investment under deflation

6 November 1962

---

'I know something about deflation. I graduated in 1930. Since my main interest in life at that period was trying to keep off the bread-line I wasn't particularly interested in the stock market so I would be interested to know how markets behaved in the inter-war period or how deflation affected them.'

---

JOURNALISTS are a funny lot. At times, having written a piece, they feel as Moses must have felt when he got the tablets to the bottom of the mountain. At times, they go to the opposite extreme and assume that a subject is so well known there's no point in writing about it. Letters, such as the one from which I quote above, which I received as a result of my recent article 'Please, What is Deflation?' are a great help in maintaining perspective.

To describe the events of 22 years in one short article is a bit of a tall order. What I propose to do in answer to my reader, therefore, is to give you my main impressions of the investment scene of 1918–1939. Looking back over that period, I suppose the most striking recollection is what a static place the London Stock Exchange was.

That may seem a strange thing to say of an era which contained three booms and two slumps (with another uncompleted slump which culminated in the summer of 1940). Yet it was true in the sense that the Duke of York's men, although they marched up the hill and down again, remained on the hill all the time. Ordinary shares as a group in the inter-war period doubled and then halved in value – more or less – with a regularity which carried its own fascination.

I'm not referring so much to the brief and hectic boom and slump which occurred in the immediate post-First War years, as to the pattern of boom, slump, boom, slump which ran through the 'twenties and 'thirties and which, ironically enough, left the London and Cambridge share index in 1940 almost exactly where it had been in 1918.

The background to all this, of course, was the fact that Britain really *was* a stagnant society then. The figures for our national income during the period shown in my chart (at the prices of 1900

86

throughout) are those compiled by Dr A. R. Prest in an article in the *Economic Journal* of March, 1948. They show that it was only towards the end of the period that the British economy grew at all. Even so, given the tremendous housing boom and the rearmament programme of the 'thirties, a growth of some 18 per cent spread over 19 years wasn't much to shout about.

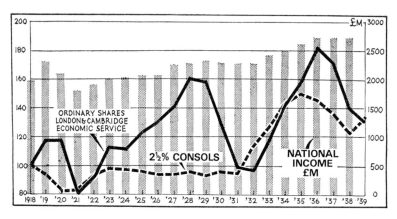

This is not to say that there weren't jolly good growth stocks in those years. A hundred pounds invested in Cerebos in 1924 was worth about £1,750 in 1938; the same amount in Tillings (then purely a bus concern) grew to £900 over the same period; the value of GEC shares rose five-fold. (There's a moral in that somewhere for GEC share-holders to-day.) But such shares were darned difficult to find. Neither Courtaulds nor EMI, for all that rayon and disc shares were all the rage, succeeded in beating the index – or Old Consols for that matter.

As a result of this, the vogue of investment timing became as fashionable as the vogue of growth has been in recent years. The whole art then was to get into equities at the bottom of a cycle and out of them, either into gilt-edged or building societies, at the top. Until quite recently, it hasn't mattered buying into equities as a class at the top of any of the post-Second War booms; you just had to wait until a new Chancellor of the Exchequer was appointed and he duly floated you off. (Mr Maudling, please note.)

It was very different between the wars. It has been calculated, for example, that if an investor had switched from 2½ per cent Consols into equities in January, 1929, he would have had to wait as long as 23 years before the capital value of the money had it been left in Consols would have been overtaken (ignoring interest income and expenses).

Timing wasn't only fashionable; it was vital. Ironically enough, some schemes aimed at perfecting timing techniques were worked out to coincide almost exactly with the disappearance of these major cyclical movements. One of my fondest recollections of the period, parenthetically, is of the investor who bought equities when the National Government was formed in September 1931, because that was what the authors of *1066 and All That* would have called a Good Thing, and sold when Edward abdicated in December, 1936, because that was what they would have called a Bad Thing. It wasn't very scientific but it was magnificent timing.

It wasn't only timing that was vital. In the new issue boom of 1928, 284 companies were floated. Within less than three years, nearly one-third of these companies had either been wound up or had no ascertainable value. Old established concerns, companies on which Britain's prosperity had been built in the nineteenth century, underwent capital reconstruction after capital reconstruction, with their prior charges written off almost to nothing and their equity capitals cut to nominal amounts. (Not that this latter operation signified anything in real terms in the long run, unless a lot of the equity had to be ceded to the prior charge holders, as did happen quite often.)

The Board of Trade of those days opposed full disclosure in shipping accounts on the grounds that if our competitors had known just how close to bankruptcy our leading companies were they would have put them out of business within two years. By the way, someone told me the other day that only four public companies with a capital of £1 million or more had gone into liquidation since 1945.

It was conditions such as these, of course, as well as the appreciation in the purchasing power of the pound I was discussing in my previous article, and the conscious use of cheap money after 1931, although not in a Daltonian sense, which gave high class fixed interest stocks their very considerable investment status throughout most of the inter-war years, particularly in the 'thirties, when it is also clear that the rise in gilt-edged helped equity share values considerably. Statistics on the market's yield structure for this period are limited.

But it seems very doubtful whether a 'reverse yield gap' – the state of affairs in which equities yield less than, say, Old Consols – existed more than momentarily during the inter-war years. There is some evidence to show that during the boom of 1920, equity yields were on a parity with the yield on 2½ per cent Consols, and I believe that for one month at the beginning of the recovery in trade in 1932 the Actuaries Ordinary share index was actually yielding less than gilt-edged. But by and large equities *always* yielded more than gilt-edged.

In fact, however, dividend income on a well-spread portfolio of equities was rising slowly but fairly steadily throughout most of the period. Mind you, there were setbacks, notably between 1920 and 1922 and again between 1929 and 1932; in the former period, there is evidence to show that dividends on blue chips fell by 20 per cent and in the latter period the fall was about 35 per cent. The institutional investor seems to have been more concerned with these periods of setback – and, of course, the sharp swings in capital values and the bitter experiences of company mortalities – than with the slow but quite substantial overall rise in equity dividends. For in fact, investment and unit trusts apart, only a tiny handful of institutional investors – mainly insurance companies, for pension funds were almost non-existent then – were dashing enough to buy any equity shares, and some of those went through some very worrying periods soon after they started on their great adventure.

Well, there we are. I hope this brief account of the broad experiences of investors in the inter-war years may be of some interest to those of you who, like my correspondent, had no first-hand experience of it. As one who lived pretty close to this canvas during most of the period the artists were working on it, I can only conclude on much the same note as that on which I finished 'Please, What is Deflation?' The pundits may be right and we may be in danger of moving into a deflationary era. But I can't help feeling that any real resemblance between the period we have been discussing and that which lies ahead will be purely accidental.

# Taxing gilt-edged capital gains

5 January 1965

MR Callaghan's tax proposals, we are told, can be justified because other countries do likewise. Well, people in other
countries live in igloos, practise polygamy, or wear topless
dresses, but we don't accept this as justification for doing those
things in Britain. I want to examine the proposition with particular
reference to the decision that the proposed capital gains tax should
apply to the gilt-edged market, subject to the possibility that the
Chancellor may, in the fullness of time, decide to exempt certain
investors from the tax.

There can be no doubt that if the justification for this decision of
Mr Callaghan's is to be found in what other countries do, the country
most people have in mind is the United States, which, of course, has
taxed capital gains for 50 years, and includes in those gains redemption 'profits' on Government bonds.

I do not propose to debate here whether or not the fulfilment of a
contract to redeem an obligation does indeed create 'profit'. But I
thought it might be worth while seeing whether one really can compare the British and American gilt-edged markets.

What we are comparing are the marketable central Government
securities of both countries, from bills to long-dated and (in the case
of Britain) irredeemable stocks. My sources are, for the UK, the
Financial Statement issued at the time of the Budget, and the
statistical bulletin of the Federal Reserve System in Washington.

The first thing that has to be said is that, relatively speaking, the
American Government bond market is chicken-feed. The total of
£22,580 million of British obligations equals some 75 per cent of our
gross national product; the American total of $208,009 million
represents some 36 per cent of their GNP. (There is scope for a lot of
hard thinking about the financial and economic consequences of this
comparison, but we needn't go into that.)

This apart, the thing that positively shrieks aloud when you look
at the figures is the utterly different structure of the two gilt-edged
markets. Of the American marketable securities, as much as 70 per
cent is redeemable within five years, and as much as 88 per cent
within ten years, leaving only 12 per cent which can be described as
medium or long term. Here, only 43 per cent of our total is reedemable

within five years, and only 54 per cent within ten. As much as 31 per cent (against 8 per cent in America) has a life of over 20 years or need never be redeemed.

This heavy concentration of short-term debt has, of course, been a source of constant worry to conservative Americans. I recall that in 1957 Mr George Humphrey, on retiring as Secretary of the Treasury, said that he inherited a mess, and was passing on a mess to his successor. What Mr Humphrey had in mind was the failure of all his efforts to fund more of America's debt; to get rid of this reliance on short-dated stocks.

Well, maybe Mr Humphrey worried unnecessarily. America hasn't exactly gone to pot since 1957, her heavy short-term debt notwithstanding. But in the context of the present discussion, what is important of course is that the shorter your debt the less chance there is of your securities falling much below the redemption price. Whether or not the 'profit' on redemption is subject to a capital gains tax is consequently not nearly as important as it is in a country which has a great packet of long-term and irredeemable debt, much of which was issued when interest rates were very much lower than they are to-day.

Interest rates have, admittedly, risen in America over the post-war period, just as they have risen here. But they have not risen nearly as much. The yield on long-term taxable bonds there was 2.34 per cent in 1945; in 1963 it was 4.02 per cent, an increase of 70 per cent. The mean yield on $2\frac{1}{2}$ per cent Consols here over the same period has gone up from 2.9 per cent to 5.6 per cent, a rise of 93 per cent. Reflecting all this, British Gas 3 per cent, 1990–95, stands at 58; US 3 per cents, 1995, stand around $85\frac{1}{4}$. You see what I mean about the relative importance of redemption 'profits'?

But this is not all, by a long chalk. In a recent article here (which caused a certain amount of interest) I pointed out to Mr Callaghan that he could not just say that because America's got a capital gains tax a similar tax would be O.K. here, without going into such questions as the development and the true impact of the American tax. One of the points I made was that the top income tax rate in America had come down from 91 to 77 per cent (and is due to come down to 70 per cent), and that 'even these rates do not mean much in a country where wealthy people can, for example, own tax-exempt bonds on which they pay no income-tax whatsoever'.

The fact is that, apart from the market in US Government marketable securities which we have been discussing, there is another gilt-edged market in America – the enormous and steadily growing market in tax-exempt State and local government securities. In 1963, these borrowers made issues involving new capital to the tune of $9,151 million, which happened to be in excess of the total issues involving new capital made by the US Government itself and its agencies.

You can get some idea of the growth in and the pressures on this secondary, tax-exempt, gilt-edged market when I tell you that the yield on the 'Bond Buyer's' index of 20 municipal bonds has risen from 1.42 per cent in 1945 to 3.26 per cent in 1963, an increase of 130 per cent, compared with the rise of 70 per cent in the official long-term rate. These bonds to-day give a return equivalent to 6 per cent to the taxpayer liable to tax at the 48 per cent rate and to around double figures to a 70 per cent taxpayer.

The results of this, to us, peculiar state of affairs are positively Gilbertian. It is broadly true to say that in America to-day, taxable bonds are taken up by the commercial banks and the tax-exempt institutions, while the tax-liable investor buys only tax-exempt bonds.

In these circumstances, what relevance the fact that in America the redemption 'profits' on gilt-edged are subject to the capital gains tax has to Mr Callaghan's proposal that such 'profits' here should be subject to his capital gains tax may be clear to Mr Callaghan and his advisers but eludes me.

In fact, of course, the proposition is not only silly but could be immensely damaging. American insurance companies are, as we know, much more restricted in their investment activities than their counterparts here; their holdings of equities are relatively tiny. Despite this, the 'Fed' bulletin shows that of this total of over $208,000 million of official marketable US gilt-edged securities the insurance companies held only 4.3 per cent. Here, with much greater freedom and with much larger holdings of equities, our insurance companies hold £1,605 million, or 7 per cent, of the total of £22,894 million of marketable gilt-edged paper. They are, indeed, a mainstay of our long-term gilt-edged market.

In sum, the idea that, because America's capital gains tax embraces gilt-edged redemption 'profits', our tax should do so is so ludicrous that we are forced to look elsewhere for the motives behind Mr Callaghan's original ideas. How could Mr Callaghan have been so misguided as even to contemplate taxing such 'profits'?

# Investment: home and overseas

22 February 1966

'I certainly am not aware of any instances of British industry being deprived of capital because it has been invested abroad.'

*Lord Cromer at the recent Overseas Bankers Club dinner*

YOU may find it hard to believe but generally when I start writing these articles I have a pretty good idea where they will end and how they will get there. But not this one. This, in the modern phrase, is an open-ended affair. We shall just have to see how it goes.

The starting point is the assertion that if a country does not invest abroad, it will have that much extra resources to invest at home, and will in consequence be better off. This is not an argument that has suddenly gained currency since October 1964. We have heard it for decades.

It seems to be so obvious an argument as to be hardly worth debating, and it seems particularly obvious in the case of Britain which so often lags behind its competitors in capital formation; hence the tattiness of so much of our society to-day.

My chart is not uninteresting in this connection. It gives the picture in 1964 of gross fixed assets formation as a percentage of gross national product; the figures come from the OECD Observer. We don't stand very high in this league, although, as we shall see later, 1964 was, for us, a vintage year for domestic capital formation.

It's true, of course, that countries such as Italy and Japan *need* a higher capital formation than we do. Their GNP (at current market prices and exchange rates) equals $970 and $710 per capita, compared with $1,700 for ours.

But France and Germany have both a higher capital formation and a higher GNP per head ($1,820 and $1,780 respectively) than we do. The US, where capital formation (if these figures are to be believed) is about the same as ours relative to her GNP, is, of course, so rich, with a GNP per head almost double that of any other country's, as to be a special case.

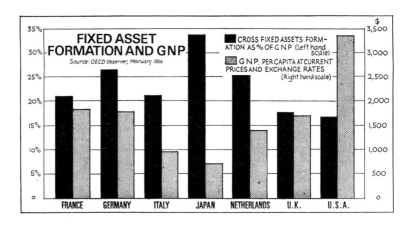

The US apart, at first glance one would say that none of the other countries in my table is a substantial foreign investor, which seems to reinforce the doctrine we are discussing. That is too facile. The world-wide success of Volkswagen was not achieved without a good deal of investment outside Germany. French investment and aid overseas have been on a very large scale, much larger than ours, in recent years and, interestingly enough, French economists have blamed the shortage of schools and new houses in France, the backwardness of Brittany, on this outflow of funds.

Nevertheless, it is indisputable that we are traditionally a large direct investor overseas and so we come back to the original proposition. We also come back to Lord Cromer's remark quoted at the beginning of this article. And I believe that anyone with practical experience of the City and industry would agree with what Lord Cromer said.

This is not to say that the City and industry do not from time to time fall down on their job. Of course they do. I had a long talk last week with the chaps who run the National Research Development

Corporation, which seems to be a very happy combination of the public and private sectors and which, among other things, took over the development of the hovercraft when the original private enterprise backers had had enough, and has put up to £5 million behind International Computers and Tabulators, which ICT might have found difficult to get elsewhere.

But Lord Cromer was not arguing that British industry and the City never made mistakes in investment decisions. He was just saying that there was no evidence to show that investment at home had been starved because of investment abroad. And, in effect, he went on to argue that, balance of payments considerations on one side, we would not command success in domestic investment just by cutting down on investment overseas.

'I have constantly been surprised', he said, 'that the aggregate new investment in industry in this country, which has been very substantial over recent years, has not produced more output'.

Certainly, when you realise that our gross domestic fixed capital formation rose from £4,912 million in 1963 to £5,800 million in 1964, an increase of no less than 18 per cent, it's a bit shattering to find that index of industrial production last December, at 133 (1958 = 100) just managed to regain the January, 1965, level, and, taking the whole of 1965, was but $2\frac{1}{2}$ per cent over the 1964 average.

Last year was, of course, a holding-back year for Britain. But on the evidence, not just of 1965 but over a much longer period, it does seem facile to assume that as we cut down on overseas investment we shall automatically transform the *quality* of our domestic investment programme, so that, enlarged though it may be, it brings the increase in productivity and wealth it ought to produce.

It seems to me that the questions we ought to be asking ourselves are not so much those relating to the profitability of our overseas investments and whether we can afford them, but those concerning the profitability (which is a non-U word for efficiency) of our domestic investments, and whether, when we have made home investment profitable and efficient, we shall not be so much richer that overseas investment will be seen to be what it was here last century and has been in the United States this – a spilling over of an abundantly filled cornucopia.

In this question of domestic investment, one has to differentiate between the public and the private sectors not on doctrinaire lines but because there are obvious limits to unprofitable investment in the latter but precious few which are discernible in the former.

I recently heard Sir Paul Chambers pointing out the economic consequences of nationalisation in the coal mining industry. If the mines were owned separately, he said, pits that were unprofitable and could not increase their productivity would have gone under. The capital invested in the industry could then have been concentrated on the economic mines, and would obviously have been much more fruitful. How much capital has been wasted in coal; how profitable has the investment in liner trains been?

We are not alone in this mis-investment in the public sector but certainly we must have suffered from it more than most comparable countries.

But no-one could argue that investment in the private sector in Britain is as profitable or efficient overall as it could or should be; George Cyriax was reminding us in his article in *The Financial Times* on 10 February of the higher returns on capital employed secured by most UK subsidiaries of US corporations compared with their opposite numbers here.

The reasons for all this are many and deep-rooted. Too much protection, too many restrictive practices all round, insufficient incentives, overfull employment, governments which are too timorous to do what they know must be done, mediocre standards in reporting on the results of investment, and above all, I suspect, our besetting sin of thinking profits and dividends to be immoral.

As and when we get rid of all these inhibiting factors and attitudes, we shall find that the scope in the domestic economy is so enormous that we can stop carping about the 'burden' of overseas investment. Equally, unless we put these things right, the present campaign against such investment will serve no useful purpose.

We don't need to be theoretical about this. Last May, Sir Cyril Harrison, chairman of English Sewing Cotton said that because of the 1965 Finance Act, ESC would be curbing its investments overseas, which he thought would be welcome news to the company's competitors in the US, Germany and Japan.

Last week, Sir Cyril compared the company's operations with identical machines in the United States and Lancashire. There, the machines are worked 144 hours each week, 51 weeks a year, with 100 per cent staff attendance. Here, there is a 49-week year, 10 per cent

Investment and Finance

absenteeism, machines are idle for lack of labour, and are only operated 100 hours a week. There, production per man hour is more than twice ours. For a given investment, the US plant produces 150 hours for every 100 in Lancashire.

Has the cut-back in ESC's overseas investment helped to makes its domestic investment more profitable?

# Parkinson's law on equities

26 April 1966

LAST week we were looking at that fascinating record of equity share prices since 1919 published by Messrs de Zoete and Gorton. As I roughed out last week's chart and came to the period from 1935 onwards, I felt on familiar ground, for more than once I have shown in these articles that, when you allow for the rise in the cost of living, there has been no rise in the FT 30 share index, in real terms, since it started in July, 1935.

After the article appeared, something said 'Take another look'. And indeed we should. Here is a unique 47-year record of equity investment in paper terms, giving not only capital values but income as well. But the paper of 1919 was avocado pears, the paper of 1933 blackcurrants and the paper of 1966 is – well, let's call it a lemon.

Avocado pears, blackcurrants and lemons may all be fruit, but they're not really comparable, are they? So I set out the cost of living figures and de Zoete and Gorton's share value and income figures year by year since 1919; where necessary converted them so that 1919 equalled 100; and then divided the share value and income figures each year by that year's cost of living figure.

The results are set out in the accompanying charts, and fascinating indeed they are. Let's take capital values first. The solid line, the paper value line, you'll recognise easily enough – it appeared on last week's chart. The dotted line is the avocado pear line.

The period covered by the chart divides itself almost exactly into halves – the non-inflationary, at times strongly deflationary half; and the inflationary half. Taking 1919 as equalling 100, the cost of living rose to 114 in 1920; it was 104 in 1921. It was 1943 before the

97

index again exceeded 100. Between 1943 and to-day, it has risen from 102 to 241.

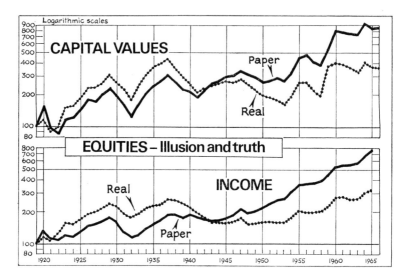

Now we're always being told that inflation's good for equities. We're always being told that the inter-war years were years of stagnation and no growth, whereas in the post-war period, for all our faults, we've seen tremendous growth.

Well, so we have, but on the evidence of this chart that tremendous growth has brought no benefit in real terms to equity capital values. It is the most astonishing thing, surely, that on my corrected figures, the holder of this fund was better off in 1937 than he was at the peak of the post-war equity rise in 1964.

'Better off?' Well, let me quote to you what Hargreaves Parkinson said in his book 'Ordinary Shares', when he was discussing an earlier but similar phenomenon his researches threw up:

'It is clear', he wrote, 'that "uncorrected" Ordinary share values failed to keep pace with the rise in prices during the decade and a half before the First Great War. At almost any time from the beginning of this century, up to the war years [1914–18] . . . whatever a representative holding of Ordinary shares might be worth in terms of money, the proceeds of a sale in the market would have bought progressively less of other things than shares'.

It took the bad old days of the 'twenties and 'thirties, the days when the purchasing power of money was rising, to allow the proceeds of a sale of shares to buy progressively more of other things than shares. Since 1943, 'HP's' earlier discovery has manifested itself in very striking fashion. The whole of the post-war rise in these paper equity values has not been sufficient to maintain the real position reached nearly thirty years ago.

When we express income in real terms, interestingly enough, the picture is different. The rise in paper incomes since 1943 *has* been sufficient and more than sufficient to offset the rise in the cost of living. One can only presume that it is the rise in interest rates during the last 30 years – they have more than doubled – that has prevented the improvement in incomes in real terms from being reflected in a corresponding improvement in capital values in real terms.

However, this improvement in income in real terms has also to be corrected for the rise in income tax over the period. In the first half, standard rates of income tax were between 20 and 30 per cent. In the second half, they have been between 40 and 50 per cent. The net yield on this equity portfolio in 1925 was 4.3 per cent; the net return in 1965 was 3.1 per cent. (The gross yields in the two years were 5.4 per cent and 5.2 per cent respectively.)

We should be quite clear what this exercise is saying. It is based on a limited but nevertheless important cross-section of Britain's biggest companies. It does not in any degree destroy the argument that over the long term equities are the best practical investment media available to the ordinary man and the ordinary institution.

The holder of this equity portfolio may have calculated that every £100 invested in 1919 is really worth to-day, not the £863 paper value he may have thought it was, but only £358 when he has allowed for the rise in the cost of living. But the £100 put into Consols in 1919 to-day would only have £27.2 worth of real purchasing power.

The equity investor has more than trebled his real (gross) income. The poor soul who stuck to Consols has seen his real (gross) income slashed by nearly 60 per cent; where £1,000 produced a real (gross) income of £42 in 1919, to-day the comparable figure in real terms is £17 10s.

But these clear investment lessons should not be allowed to obscure certain other very important lessons which the illusion of inflation tends to hide. Even allowing for the influence of the rise in interest rates, it does seem very extraordinary that the real worth of the market capitalisations of the equity of this important cross-section of Britain's biggest companies should to-day be lower than it was in 1937.

We seem to have had a very poor return for all the millions of new capital these concerns have put into their businesses by way of ploughed-back profits and new capital issues over the last three decades. Is this not pretty strong presumptive evidence that there is indeed something very badly wrong with British industry?

Secondly, on this showing, should not investors (and their advisers) stop thinking that inflation is a Good Thing? No one wants to see a return to the conditions which obtained in the 'twenties and 'thirties. But who can doubt that these companies would have done much better with stable money than they have in fact done with the inflation which everyone, in their heart of hearts, believes to be beneficial? Even the rise in interest rates (which has itself held equity values back) is, of course, an inevitable accompaniment of inflation. If we stopped inflation, and could have a long-term interest rate of 5 per cent, where would that put the FT index?

Finally, does not this exercise demonstrate beyond any shadow of doubt that unless we mend our ways, and Ordinary share values reflect true capital appreciation and not fictitious inflationary appreciation, Mr Callaghan's capital gains tax is in fact a capital levy?

The Parkinson's Law of 1944, as we have seen, laid down that every time you sold Ordinary shares between 1900 and 1914 (when, of course, there was no capital gains tax) the proceeds bought progressively less of the things the companies make.

My chart shows the process has continued since then; that in fact we already had a long-term capital gains tax – inflation itself – before last year's Finance Act. On the record of the last 47 years, now inevitably to be made worse by Mr Callaghan's additional capital levy, is it really very surprising that capitalism, or free enterprise, or whatever you like to call it, doesn't work very well in Britain?

# Making good use of deflation

26 July 1966

WE should be quite clear in our minds what happened last Wednesday (20 July). I can best express it by saying that the London School of Economics won the day, and the older foundations at Oxford and Cambridge lost it; that the Institute of Economic Affairs triumphed over Chatham House.

Whether the Prime Minister's programme is right or wrong, he showed great courage in launching it. Threats of resignations or actual resignations there may have been and may be. But as and when this deflation bites, there can be no night of the long knives in the Cabinet in an attempt to restore the Government's popularity. This will go down in history as Mr Wilson's, not Mr Callaghan's, deflation.

The programme itself is inevitably fuzzy and indeterminate – inevitably because it was thrown together in a great hurry. The figures it contains will almost certainly be proved wrong – either because the economies will not be achieved, or because it will be savings rather than spendings which are reduced, or because price control will continue to be more effective than incomes control.

The programme is marred by ritual – the absence of any attempt to rationalise the State welfare schemes; the refusal to abandon steel nationalisation; the swipe, through the surtax surcharge, at 'the wealthy'; the ceiling on company dividends, which must mean an overall *reduction* in dividend income. Sadly, these things surprise no one in this country any more. But if Mr Wilson was really out to reassure opinion overseas, these acts of omission or commission are inexplicable.

The wages freeze not only reveals a lack of confidence in the efficacy of the other measures, and the earlier ones, such as the decision not to allow the banks to finance SET. It is unjust and unrealistic. The prime and obvious victims will be the employees in the public sector under the Government's direct control, and those members of the trade union movement whose leaders support it.

We tend to forget at such moments that wages account for less than 40 per cent of total personal incomes, and that only one-third of our working population of over 25 million belongs to unions affiliated to the TUC. To believe that we can freeze all other incomes by exhortation or even legislation is self-delusion.

# The Business of Capitalism

Moreover, even if we could, what about all the productivity agreements which have been and are being painfully negotiated? Surely in such agreements, where the benefits of increased efficiency are shared between companies, workers and the community, our best hopes lie.

Nevertheless, despite all these reservations, the fact remains that Mr Wilson acted with courage and fortitude. For in essence he has repudiated the philosophy of his party since it became a political force in this country.

He has accepted that, given the traditional habits of the British people – managements and workers alike – it is impossible to run the country with no unemployment whatsoever (when you allow for the unemployables and the short-term unemployment inherent in the changing of jobs). He has dropped the pretence that, given an official unemployment rate of less than 2 per cent, we can get the redisposition of resources we must have by exhortation and gimmickry.

Instead, however fuzzy and indeterminate the programme may be, it is now clear that either Mr Wilson goes ahead with his deflationary measures, and deliberately creates more unemployment, or sterling devalues itself, which would surely mean the end of Mr Wilson.

For myself, as you may know, I have consistently argued that the policy Mr Wilson is now adopting is the right one. But I have never pretended – and I am sure that Mr Wilson would never pretend – that in a programme such as the one Labour has evolved over the last few weeks lies any permanent cure to our troubles.

Last week's package is essentially negative. It should reduce the overheating in the economy. It should cut our imports, and hence put our payments position in balance. It should moderate the rise in incomes and prices as the extreme pressures in the labour market diminish.

But none of this will solve our basic and self-evident dilemma, which I have described in the sentence: 'We daren't expand; to contract is ineffective'. On expansion, the proposition is self-evident. On contraction, I reproduce an up-to-date version of a chart which appeared here over a year ago, which provides clear enough evidence that neither Mr Selwyn Lloyd's deflation, which did create unemployment, nor Mr Callaghan's, which didn't, was effective. The contraction we now face *must* be made effective. How?

President Johnson, I see, has been pointing out that in America wages and fringe benefits have marched broadly in step since 1960 with productivity; that 'the American worker's standard of living has improved far faster than that of his British friend'. President Johnson suggests that the lesson is that 'rapid growth and freedom requires steady self-discipline and restraint.'

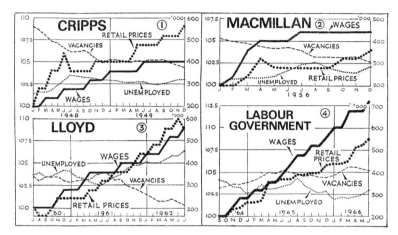

With great respect, I suggest that 'steady self-discipline and re-straint' have had nothing to do with the American performance. What has done the trick there has been a much more competitive economy; sophisticated trade union leadership which bargains hard but has no hostility to profits earned competitively and through rising efficiency; real incentives to one and all; and an absence of the climate of envy and hostility towards success which, alas, exists here.

I rejoice that Mr Wilson rejected the pleas for import quotas, which clearly would have feather-bedded British industry even more. Rather am I sure that it would be wiser in the long run, instead of eating up our overseas assets in an attempt to maintain the status quo, to mobilise those assets, aggregate them with our reserves, and then deliberately, and if necessary unilaterally, cut our tariffs. (If we are in the end forced to devalue, this will become an absolute must.)

The creation of more competitive conditions here is, I submit, a terribly one-sided affair. We have made some progress since the war, through the control of monopolies and mergers, restrictive practices and price-fixing, to make management more competition-minded.

At the same time, it is clearly part of the Government's policy to encourage or force larger units in British industry. But if it is right to fine eight tyre companies £10,000 a head when they are in breach of an undertaking to the Restrictive Practices Court, why should not the union which is holding up the liner trains by its restrictive practices also be fined £10,000?

Sir Frank Kearton now has the job of encouraging rationalisation among British companies, and the steel industry is pretty obviously going to be forced into mergers. For how long must we attempt to run this country with something like 40 times the number of trade unions Western Germany has? For how long shall we tolerate the position where an industry can be crippled by a union with 70,000 members which spends over 25 per cent of its income in financing strikes in plant after plant, when the major union in that industry, with a membership of over a million, spends only 2 per cent of its income in strike benefits?

I know all about the Royal Commission on trade unions, but we didn't need Royal Commissions to make life more uncomfortable for managements.

For how long shall we be content to operate expensive plant for 70 per cent of the time and at half the production per man hour that identical machines operate and produce in the United States?

It is to this sort of question we must be addressing ourselves during the coming contraction, which at a guess will last into 1968. Is this contraction, like all the previous contractions, to be ineffective; to tantalise us, at its end, with the possibilities of an expansion we dare not carry through? Brutally, the Prime Minister's courage last week may hang him for a lamb. He might as well be hanged for a sheep – or, if you like to mix your metaphors, the whole hog, while he's at it.

# 5

# Tariffs and Taxes

# Two pounds

## 4 December 1951

'How's the article going, Dad?'
'Well, I've written the heading.'
'What's that?'
' "Two Pounds".'
'Why not "Forty Bob"?'
'Because I don't mean "Forty Shillings". I mean "Two Pounds", two different sorts of pounds.'
'You're not going to give 'em that old stuff about the fifty-seven different external values for sterling? The Heinz line?'
'I'll thank you for a little more respect, my lad. I'm not in the habit of giving them "old stuff" as you call it. What I have in mind is a philosophical dissertation on the different values attached internally to a currency in the modern Socialist State. How such differences arise, their social and economic consequences, the damage they do, and so on.'
'Cor.'
'Now if – *if* I repeat – I were to give you, as my son, five pounds as a Christmas box, they would be five dear pounds.'
'How come?'
'Will you stop using these disgusting expressions? They would be dear pounds because they would come from my net taxed income – and as you may or may not know, my net taxed income is so small that it is very precious. Very dear, in fact. But if you were my office boy and I gave you five pounds as a Christmas box, they would be cheap pounds.'
'Why?'
'Because, you dolt, the firm would charge the five pounds as expenses against their tax liability. So it would cost them only about two pounds ten. If you were office boy to a firm of wealthy and successful stockbrokers, the five pounds might cost them 2s 6d. Now do you see?'
'Any of your prosperous pals on the Stock Exchange looking for an office boy, Dad?'
'The existence of these two sharply differing internal values for our currency has a profound effect on the social values of our leading business executives. It forces them on to what may be described as

106

the "smoked-salmon-for-lunch – grilled-herring-for-supper-stand-ard".'

'Come again? Sorry – would you please develop your thesis, Father?'

'Well, most of them live on expense allowances – or other people's – during their working day. Cheap pounds. But when they come home, they're back on net, taxed income – dear pounds. Hence the herring. Hence the airy way they change the subject when their wives – who've made do on a cup of cocoa and a piece of mousetrap – ask them what they had for lunch to-day, dear. The trouble has been made worse in recent years by what are known as the "initial allowances".'

'What're they?'

'Well, if you buy something to use in your business, you're allowed to charge nearly half the cost against your tax liability in the first year.'

'So what?'

'So second-hand car values have been about twice as high as they ought to have been. So you put a television set in the boardroom and all the directors are missing when Austria plays England. So your Uncle Maurice has completely mechanised his stockbroking business. So your cousin Percy has bought new cash registers for every branch in his chain of shops. So farmers buy a lot of tractors and stuff they don't really want and can't really afford. So the inflationary pressure in the economy has been enormously increased.'

'But didn't I hear you telling Uncle Maurice the other day that these initial allowances were going to stop?'

'Yes, dear. That's why he mechanised his business, pretty darned quick. You watch what happens to second-hand car values next April.'

'But so soon as the initial allowances have stopped, E.P.T. will be in operation, won't it Dad?'

'Yes, before in fact.'

'Then the firm that's paying E.P.T. will have lots of cheap pounds. Far more even than with initial allowances. They'll charge everything 100 per cent against tax, instead of a measly 40.'

'Son, one of these days you'll go a long way. You are, if I may say so, a true product of this modern age.'

'Oh, come off it, Dad. You've got to move with the times. But go on with your disser-what-you-may-call-it.'

# The Business of Capitalism

'Well, the existence of these cheap pounds in the hands of a relatively small section of the community creates a great deal of envy, covetousness and bad feeling among what the Socialists love to call the "under-privileged" classes. You see, they tried 19s 6d surtax, dividend limitation, capital levies, almost everything they could think of. But still the boss bowled up in his Bentley to lunch at Claridges. The trade unionists didn't like it.'

'But if the boss can't have his Bentley and his lunch at Claridges, why should he bother to be boss?'

'That, son, is the crux of the matter. It's all a question of what we call "Incentive". What the *Economist* dubbed "the carrot". Because we've all got so few dear pounds, we all do our utmost to command cheap pounds. Why, Mr Attlee, who doesn't believe in financial incentives at all, made more cheap pounds for himself than any other Prime Minister in British history. Russia, strangely enough, learnt wisdom years ago. She's always used the stick. But she found the stick alone wasn't enough. So she went back to the carrot. There's a book in my study by a man called Wendell Willkie which describes what the boss in Russia gets; what he got even in war-time.'

'And what does he get, Dad?'

'The Russian equivalent of a Bentley to take him to his lunch at Claridges. Only the Russian boss gets it without any suggestion of fiddling.'

'Well, why don't we take a leaf out of the Russians' book? It seems to me that all cheap pounds do is to make people spend a lot of money on things they wouldn't otherwise buy.'

'Precisely. I couldn't have expressed it better myself. But before you can get rid of cheap pounds, you've got to reduce taxation. And before you can reduce taxation, you've got to reduce excessive government spending.'

'I see. But you haven't got very far with that article, Dad.'

'No, son. Still only the heading.'

'But it sounds like a good article. Why don't you get on with it?'

'Because I can't see how it's going to end.'

'The article, or excessive government spending?'

'Both, son.'

# "But not this week"

## 4 April 1961

TWO weeks ago I was arguing the case here for a Budget which would make our tax system less progressive than it is now. Since such a Budget could well, in a generally buoyant home market, restart a cost-push inflation (pardon my jargon) I went on to suggest that we should combat any tendency to set wages and prices rising again by a reduction in tariffs on imported goods.

Two readers wrote to the Editor of *The Financial Times*, commenting on that article. Reader Number One implicitly thought lower tariffs now not a bad idea because he recalled that 30 years ago he had pleaded for a variable tariff structure to raise or lower profits as circumstances demanded. Reader Number Two mainly feared that our reserves weren't strong enough for the experiment but also accused me, by way of an aside, of being a Keynesian.

I'm not altogether clear what a Keynesian is, but I found the juxtaposition of the two letters fascinating. For in fact 30 years ago Keynes, who had been a free trader, turned advocate of protectionism. His motive was, of course, crystal clear. He was appalled at the structural unemployment which afflicted so much of Britain, and he thought tariffs would help us to get rid of that unemployment.

More than incidentally, for so great a man he was surprisingly naive in this matter. He believed that once the scourge of mass unemployment had been conquered, and as prices began to rise, tariffs could – and would – be discarded. Prices have been rising now for 25 years; we have had overfull employment for 20. Yet even to talk of reducing tariffs, let alone abolishing them, brings goose-pimples out on people's flesh.

It seems strange indeed that in this post-war world of overfull employment we have not been more willing to reconsider the tariff policy we adopted at the beginning of the thirties in economic circumstances so utterly different from those of to-day; it might have been another world we were living in. In parentheses, it may be noted that Keynes (as Sir Roy Harrod records in his biography of the great economist) did not want both protection *and* devaluation, even in the grim days of the world economic blizzard. When we went off gold, he wrote to *The Times* urging that consideration of the tariff question should be deferred.

# The Business of Capitalism

Ever since Dr Dalton resigned, we have been seeking the answer to the problem of how to combine full employment, growth and stable prices. We have revived the use of the interest rate weapon; we have tried fiscal policy, even to the extent of having two Budgets in one year sometimes; we have varied exchange rates; we have introduced hire purchase controls and the special deposit system for our banks, neither of which we used before the war; we have clapped on a rigorous foreign exchange control. Demonstrably, none of these – or even all of them in combination – have given us our heart's desire. Yet probably the most powerful aid of all in increasing competition, keeping prices down and putting an automatic brake on profits and wages, we have hardly used at all.

There are presumably two reasons for this – if we are not so cynical as to assume that we positively like overfull employment and inflation. First, we must be reluctant to reduce tariffs unilaterally when we can hope to trade our reductions against cuts elsewhere. Secondly – as the letter from Reader Number Two shows – we are fearful that any unilateral cut in tariffs must bring retribution in the shape of a balance of payments crisis. In short, the attitude even of those who regard greater competition as positively desirable is reminiscent of the soldier's letter: 'Dear Mother – I am sending you 7s 6d, but not this week'.

How soundly based is this attitude? It would seem at first blush that last week's balance of payments White Paper proves conclusively that it would be folly of the first water to do anything to encourage any further increase in imports; the overall picture portrayed there – not only for 1960 but even on the revised figures for earlier years – is pretty grim. Yet the very grimness of the picture rubs in the inadequacies of the policies adopted so far. Desperate situations call for desperate remedies. Secondly, if we are to adopt import liberalisation as a conscious spur to British industry to make itself better able to compete in foreign markets – at the same moment that we are presumably offering our businessmen real incentive to export – there are worse times to do so than at the end of a year in which imports have risen by £500 million. This is particularly true when analysis of that record import bill shows that a large part of the rise in imports was not in 'frivolous' items but in fact represented stockpiling of raw materials and supplies of the tools on which a successful export drive must be launched.

I question whether even the increase in 'frivolous' imports (the quotation marks are deliberate; I do not set myself up as a judge of frivolity) are permanent. I don't doubt that Detroit regarded the imports of European cars into the United States in 1959 and the early months of 1960 as 'frivolous'. But Detroit didn't just sit with its hands in its lap saying 'Goodness, how sad'. It upped and produced the sort of car the customer wanted. Equally, I don't doubt that our producers of 'frivolous' goods have been scratching their heads and bucking their ideas up to meet the competition the recent liberalisation of imports caused. We are probably benefiting even now from the pummelling these chaps received.

I'm not arguing for complete free trade. I know the weaknesses of our balance of payments and financial position as well as the next man. I believe the judicious use of the tariff weapon, by preventing a new round of wage and price increases, would improve, not jeopardise, that position. And since I am accused of being a Keynesian, may I conclude by quoting what Keynes had to say when he advocated the abandonment of free trade in 1931?

'I have reached my own conclusion as the result of continuous reflection over many months, without enthusiasm, as the result of the gradual elimination of the practical alternatives as being more undesirable. . . . I seem to see the elder parrots sitting round and saying: "You can rely on us. Every day for 30 years, regardless of the weather, we have said 'What a lovely morning!' But this is a bad bird. He says one thing one day, and something else the next".'

By a strange coincidence, those last words appeared in the *New Statesman* exactly 30 years ago to-day. Let their advocacy of protection then stand in support of a plea for freer trade now.

# Why not a selective pay-roll tax?

25 February 1964

I HAD no idea when I wrote that article, 'Do the British Really Want to Grow?' seven short weeks ago that the question would become actual so soon. Indeed, I recorded 'the unanimity with which all the pundits, in discussing the economic prospects for 1964, have decided that we shall have to put the brakes on during the *second* half of the year'.

# The Business of Capitalism

As everyone knows, two things have caused discussion of the process of brake-application to be advanced by at least six months – the January trade returns and the 10 February unemployment figures. By general consent, it is the second of these which is the more worrying.

I have no quarrel with this assessment. We have the reserves and the borrowing powers to see us through any temporary balance of payments deficit caused by industrial re-stocking of raw materials. I don't think the foreigner would bat an eyelid if we used those reserves and powers, provided he was satisfied that history wasn't going to repeat itself on the second count.

On this, some commentators have short memories. One of them said last week that 'another credit squeeze or a *second* pay pause (my italics) would make everyone writhe'. God bless my soul. Didn't Sir Stafford Cripps have a pay pause in 1949? Wasn't that 1951 Budget of Hugh Gaitskell's I was describing the other week designed to enforce not just a pay pause but an actual cut in real wages? Didn't Mr Macmillan, when he was Chancellor of the Exchequer, keep exhorting the unions to moderate their demands and industrialists to keep profits down?

The fact is – and Heaven knows I've been hammering away at it for years and years – that when unemployment falls below a certain level and the number of jobs vacant rises above that level, we lose all control of incomes and our costs go to pot. This is what worries the foreigner. When the process starts, he doesn't want to hold pounds. And when the Governor of his Central Bank agrees to put up the funds to help him get out of pounds, the Governor not unnaturally insists that somehow or other we get our costs back under control.

The foreigner of course has had similar worries in his own country in recent times, and we have comforted ourselves that we have held our costs down much more successfully than he has. This is true in a way. But when it comes to export prices, as my chart shows, we haven't done so well even at a time when we've held internal costs reasonably steady. What happens if internal costs really jump?

The point of my article seven weeks ago was to suggest that we didn't have to sit hopeless and helpless while the whole thing came to pieces in our hands yet again. I have been fascinated to read all the best commentators – not the mere buffoons of growthmanship – busily trotting out all the old remedies; a higher Bank Rate, 3*d* a packet on cigarettes, a Budget which subtracts £200 million or so from total personal incomes which must now be around £25,000 million a year.

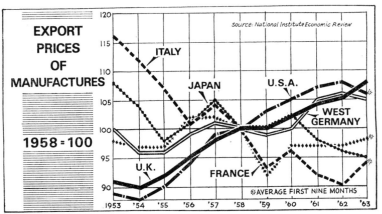

Mind you, I'm not against these things. But really, they're fiddling, temporary expedients. They do nothing whatsoever to touch the fundamental troubles of the British economy, which go back sixty years or more – an industry which is insufficiently competitive; a labour force which is badly disposed, under-employed (whatever the official figures show) and riddled with restrictive practices; and a general attitude of mind which is quite happy to doddle along with things as they are.

For the last twelve years, in the main, we've just inflated, deflated and reflated without really attempting to tackle these fundamental ills. (Under the Labour Government there wasn't any need to inflate, although Dalton did, but equally the problems weren't tackled.)

Seven weeks ago I suggested certain things we could do if we wanted to demonstrate to the world that we were in earnest in our protestations that we do indeed want good and steady growth. For example, that we should open our shores to immigrants and drastic-ally revise our definitions of skilled labour; abolish RPM and reduce tariffs where an industry was judged to be charging too much; take a new look at our fuel and energy policies; make the Monopolies Commission an effective body; toughen up our attitudes to wage increases, not least in the public sector.

# The Business of Capitalism

Some of these suggestions made some of you so angry that they confirmed my suspicion that some of you don't really want us to grow. Two or possibly three of the ideas have been or are on their way to being adopted. Now I want to throw out another suggestion, at least for serious examination.

This idea rests on two propositions. The first is that in fact we have plenty of manpower but that we don't use it properly. Industrial consultants with experience outside this country know this; our industrialists who study their overseas competitors know it – I see Mr Paul Chambers was saying last week that in the US it takes half the number of people to run a plant that it does here; even newspapermen who read their Shawcross know it.

The second proposition is that if we are stopped in our tracks this coming summer or autumn it will be because the Midlands and London and the South-east are overheated while the rest of the country is not. This again is a familiar picture and we know from experience, given our trade union and industrial structure, that overheating in these areas affects the whole country's costs.

My suggestion is that the Government should take from its pigeon-hole Selwyn Lloyd's idea of a pay-roll tax put forward in April, 1961. That tax, you may remember, was still-born. But it aroused a good deal of discussion. Some people liked the idea; some people hated it. Some thought it would have no effect; some thought it would have too much.

In fact, the Government itself seems to have been a bit confused about the whole thing. It was coupled with the new power to vary consumption taxes outside the Budget, as an economic regulator and revenue raiser. Clearly, it would have affected adversely all profits – of efficient as well as inefficient companies – yet it was associated with an increase in profits tax and a refusal to do anything about the fuel duty. (The latter was actually increased three months later in the 'little budget'.) It would have applied in the areas of high unemployment as well as in the prosperous parts of the country.

The idea that I think is worth exploring is the use of a pay-roll tax, the incidence of which would vary plant by plant from nil in the areas of high unemployment to a maximum in the areas which are, or will soon be, overheated. This, I agree, is frank discrimination, but if the whole country's growth is going to be jeopardised because certain areas are overheated, discrimination seems justified.

114

The trade unions were hotly opposed to the pay-roll tax in the form Selwyn Lloyd put it forward. In the revised form, I don't see why they should be. Even in London, the South East and the Midlands, there is waste of manpower which a pay-roll tax must help to cure. And in the nature of things labour shaken loose in these areas would have little or no difficulty in finding other jobs.

Moreover, instead of using the money produced by the tax for general revenue purposes – Selwyn Lloyd's tax, it was estimated, would yield about £100 million a year net – I would like to see it set aside in a special fund, the proceeds of which would be used only to encourage labour mobility and efficiency by providing for reasonable severance pay, re-training facilities, improved apprenticeship schemes and so on. If this were done, so far from making workers more insecure, the tax would go a long way towards increasing their security.

Well, you can say once again I'm talking rubbish. You can go on suggesting adjustments in Bank Rate, a tax on betting, tuppence on this and threepence on that, but don't tell me these things are going to solve our basic problems, put us on the road for good and sustained growth. The way to growth is through incentives to investment and penalties when that investment isn't used efficiently; the old idea of the carrot and the stick, in fact. We've tried the carrot – which isn't to say we couldn't have bigger and better carrots. What's wrong with a bit of stick to see us through until we've got a really competitive economy?

# Shall we tax or shall we save?

3 May 1966

---

'Here we have it, the cardinal dilemma of the British economy. We daren't expand. Contraction is ineffective.'

---

THESE words appeared in an article of mine something over four years ago – one day after Selwyn Lloyd had produced his 1962–63 Budget, and about a month after the Organisation for Economic Co-operation and Development had issued a report on the British economy. This report concentrated a good deal of its attention on what had up to then been our two main expansionary periods, 1953–55 and 1959–60, and discussed why they fizzled out so dismally.

Some of you then thought I was too pessimistic, too defeatist for words. Well, since that article appeared we have had another bash at expansion, and we know how that ended; and, whatever he and his colleagues may have said at the election, Mr Callaghan has been trying contraction for eighteen months, and we know how that has ended. The verdict of 11 April 1962, stands fully justified on 3 May 1966. The cardinal dilemma of the British economy remains unresolved. This is why I hope and pray that to-day the Chancellor will go bald-headed for a really massive increase in personal savings.

It has been abundantly demonstrated again and again in recent years that it is quite fallacious, given a high level of employment, to believe you can 'take purchasing power out of the economy' by increasing taxation. The public has got its own very effective defence mechanisms if you try to do so.

First, as happened last year, the British people price themselves back into the market by increasing their wages and salaries. Secondly, again as happened last year, they draw on their past savings, even in advance of the attempt to cut down their purchasing power by increasing taxation.

'In 1965', said last week's White Paper on our National Income and Expenditure, 'saving was particularly low in relation to disposable income in the first quarter when expenditure was high, *partly in anticipation of tax changes in the Budget*' (my italics). Hasn't the same thing been going on this time?

Isn't it much better in these circumstances, given the need for a reduction of $x$ hundred millions in internal purchasing power, to induce the public to do the job themselves through higher savings?

One of the greatest difficulties we have had throughout the post-war period has been in explaining to the man and the woman in the street the truth about our economic position. They really don't understand economic jargon, and they're sick and tired of hearing it. Anyway, they're baffled because the economic experts are split round down the middle. But if a really massive savings campaign was launched, on the simple proposition that if the British people save more they will be taxed less, they'd get the message all right.

My economist friends used to chuckle during the last war at some of the methods adopted 'to pay for the war'. And, of course, some of those methods were pretty quaint. We had the most regimented and controlled economy we – or for that matter any other country – had ever seen. Whatever the government wanted in the way of real resources it very properly took.

In those circumstances, it was impossible to believe that we should have gone short of a single Spitfire if wealthy people hadn't written out big cheques to pay for them, if the children hadn't contributed their few pence each week to the National Savings Movement, if old ladies hadn't given Lord Beaverbrook all their derelict aluminium saucepans.

Quaint or not, the methods enabled people, ordinary people who understood nothing about economics, to identify themselves with the supreme national effort of our history. Could not a similar, all-out effort succeed now, when a relatively small increase in personal savings would revolutionise our economic outlook?

I pointed out three weeks ago that if we could save the same percentage of personal disposable incomes as the West German people do, the result would be an increase in savings of £1,000 million. Mr Callaghan would, of course, have to use some sprats to catch his mackerel, which might reduce the gross figure quite substantially. The campaign would have to be mounted and sustained maybe for five years and the results initially might be quite modest. Obviously, too, there would be a good deal of switching of old savings to take advantage of new inducements the Chancellor offered.

But halve my figure of £1,000 million, concede that it would take a few years to build the thing up, and the benefits would still be staggering. The main impact would, of course, fall on internal consumption. That must mean lower imports and higher exports. It could well mean the end of our balance of payments troubles. It could well mean a decisive reversal of the trend, which has been going on now for some fifteen years, of ever-increasing interest rates. It would greatly moderate inflation and eventually enable taxation to be reduced.

Moreover, it would be virtually impossible to overdo the thing, as some economists fear 'deflationary' fiscal policies of the type we have become so accustomed to might be overdone. Is it really possible to talk of excessive savings in a country like ours, where there is still such a vast amount of investment to be done, both in the private and public sectors; where we have massive overseas debts to repay; and then face the need to build up our reserves, so that we could help less fortunate countries and follow a policy of cheapening imports, again as Western Germany does?

There would be need for an educational programme, of course. Some of those splendid people, the voluntary workers in the National Savings Movement, have written to me expressing their doubts about a State Unit Trust. They don't like the idea. They argue that the money subscribed to such a trust wouldn't go direct to the Government. 'You have no right to ask the 161,000 voluntary savings group secretaries to push units composed of equities which bring nothing into the Treasury's coffers', wrote one of them.

This could be a completely bi-partisan policy politically. Let the Prime Minister and the Chancellor and Opposition leaders put the simple message over on the telly, the radio and through the Press – that what matters is non-spending, rather than the particular medium one uses for saving, which is not to say, however, that the widest possible range of media should not be provided.

The National Savings Movement, industry and the City would, we can be quite sure, back the campaign to the hilt, for everyone is sick to death of the sterility of the old, dreary, restrictionist fiscal policies we have been following, year in year out, regardless of which government we elect.

The economic pundits all have their own ideas of the amount Mr Callaghan should to-day 'take out' of the economy, the whole economy – it is no use taking it out of the private sector if the public sector is to gobble up an equivalent amount. £150 million, £200 million, £300 million – you name it, they've mentioned it.

Let's keep a sense of proportion. We have a working population of 23 million. If each of those people entered into a contractual saving plan to put by a net 5s a week – call it five cigarettes a day – and stuck to it, that would produce over £250 million.

If a bundle of curvaceous chicks can persuade us all that we really should go to work on an egg, I warrant that if Mr Callaghan will give Sir Miles Thomas, Lord Shawcross and his colleagues on the Wider Share Ownership Council, industry and the City the means to induce and persuade the British people to save rather than to be taxed, they could do the job. Anyway, if they can't persuade us to cultivate good new habits, I'll wager that not even the Prime Minister will be able to exhort us into giving up our bad old habits.

# How not to reform taxes

7 June 1966

W E SHALL start our ruminations this week with some extracts
from last week's review of the National Institute of Economic and Social Research (which institute, the *Economist*
reminds us, is 'not a right wing body') on the Selective Employment
Tax:

'Obviously the administration will have to be improved; it is
rather clumsy to have one Ministry collecting it (the tax) and another
refunding it. It is unfortunate that its effect on economic activity in
general works through costs and prices.

'In time it can no doubt be made more selective. . . . It's regional
incidence is rather haphazard. . . . The region which receives most
benefit is the West Midlands, and there is a small bias against
Scotland. Neither (effect) is particularly desirable.

'There is a strong case for exempting the disabled and the elderly,
and reducing the tax on part-time workers. . . . The hotel industry
should perhaps be more favourably treated. . . .'

Despite these criticisms, the National Institute by no means
damns SET bell, book and candle. Indeed, it seems to believe that
Adam Smith, in whatever celestial institution is reserved for economists, must be nodding his approval of it.

For myself, I am not concerned here to debate the merits or demerits of SET, although I would remind you I have advocated a
selective pay-roll tax in these articles (albeit with the selectivity
governed by the degree of overful employment in various parts of the
country), and it does seem a good idea basically to switch taxation
away from making things and towards spending.

What I am concerned to do is to ask whether our methods of
instituting major tax reforms are the best and the most sensible
methods available. What I shall say is not a criticism exclusively of the
present Government, for preceding Governments have gone in for
similar tomfoolery, although what I shall say obviously has particular
point when you have a Government which prides itself on being a
radical and reforming Government, and which produces tax revolu-
tions annually.

Our present procedure is to keep major tax reforms a deathly secret
either until the Chancellor makes his Budget speech, or until the

Finance Bill is issued, and then to explode them on to an unsuspecting and baffled world.

This initial process inevitably means that the business of framing the reforms is hugged to a minimum number of bosoms. There is an intellectual arrogance inherent in the process; a reiteration of a belief in the ineffable wisdom of the gentlemen in Whitehall, Somerset House, King's College, Cambridge and points west; a denial of the contribution that the multiplicity of brains outside these corridors of power could make to the reform.

I heard the intellectual arrogance reach its apogee when I listened to Mr John Diamond, Chief Secretary to the Treasury, speaking at the *Investors Chronicle* Investment Conference last week. SET, he implied, must be a good tax because so many people had protested so violently against it. Are we to believe that the public hangings in the Congo were justified by the protests they aroused?

Then, when the Chancellor has duly exploded the bombshell, and political reputations have been involved beyond recall, begins what Mr Alun Davies has described in his recent book; *Render Unto Caesar?\**, as 'one of the most hectic rushes in British politics'.

Within four months, the Finance Bill must become law, however complicated the reforms it embodies and regardless of all the other business the House has to transact. During that period, Parliament, with a nice regard for priorities, normally takes a fortnight off for Easter and a fortnight off for Whitsun.

There are three printings of the Finance Bill, five periods for digestion and preparation, as well as time for debate, which takes at least 15 days, and sometimes a good many nights as well.

The result can be a shambles. Mr Davies quotes the immortal words of the Tory Solicitor-General (Sir Reginald Manningham-Buller, now Lord Dilhorne) during the committee stage in 1954:

'I have to admit to the Committee that my last speech was made on the wrong amendment. I am glad no one noticed it. The speech which I made on the last amendment was the one I ought to have made in moving this one'.

I rather doubt whether it would have mattered very much last year if speeches had been made on the wrong Finance Bill, or whether anyone would have noticed if they had been.

Other countries which, judged by their economic performance,

\*Elek Books, 21s net.

seem to be rather better run than Britain is, conduct their affairs very differently. I have previously commented on the way in which the Kennedy tax reforms in the United States were freely and openly debated, in congressional inquiry committees and elsewhere for many long months before they were adopted.

In Western Germany to-day a long discussion is going on about the change-over to an added-value tax on French lines. The Dutch Parliament recently took over two years discussing fundamental tax reforms. Swiss tax experts have expressed astonishment at our procedures, and their results.

I am not suggesting, of course, that there should be any change in procedure where normal, run-of-the-mill tax changes are concerned. But when fundamental reforms are involved – and goodness knows we stand in need of fundamental reforms – we might surely listen to what Mr Davies, who I suppose knows as much about tax, from both sides of the fence, as any man, has to say.

'The idea of eliminating from the annual Finance Bill tax reforms of purely technical nature, even controversial ones, has not been sufficiently discussed, and one certain way to ensure that these reforms are not allowed proper debate is to insist that they have to be carried on the jolting wagon of the hell-for-leather Finance Bill.

'There seems to be a good case for considering every few years an Income Tax Bill which would incorporate useful ideas of reform of substance and procedure and which could be discussed without the Whips having to keep an eye constantly on the clock'. I'm sure that if Mr Davies had known about SET he would have made that sentence more embracing. He is even radical enough to suggest that a properly reconstituted Upper Chamber could make its own contribution to Finance Bills, without affecting the right of the Commons to the final say in financial matters.

The Labour Party as now represented in Westminster is said to be a party anxious to modernise and reform Parliamentary procedure. It could do a lot worse than start on our archaic and unsatisfactory methods of achieving the tax reforms we all know have to come.

It cannot be right that fundamental and basically sensible tax reforms should be botched as they are under our present procedure; there were 400 amendments to last year's Finance Bill, and in this year's Bill over 40 pages are taken up with yet further amendments. It cannot be right that so much animosity and ill-will between

Government and taxpayer should be created. It cannot be right that a Government which says it cares for people should be seen to set out to penalise charities, the elderly and the disabled because they haven't thought the thing through.

# Adam Smith and you-know-who

4 October 1966

'We are not, begging Mr Gunter's pardon, an inherently dishonest and thriftless people. To the extent that we have become so, the politicians are to blame.' – *This space, last week.*

How our old friend Adam Smith must be laughing up aloft (if the Bishop of Woolwich will allow that that is where Adam now is). Getting on for 200 years ago, he (Adam, not the Bishop) laid down four principles which any tax ought to satisfy. They were equality, certainty, convenience in payment, and economy in collection. Dr Smith commented thus.

'First, the levying of it (the tax) may require a great number of officers, whose salaries may eat up the greater part of the produce of the tax.

'Secondly, it may obstruct the industry of the people, and discourage them from applying to certain branches of business which might give maintenance and employment to great multitudes.

'Thirdly, by the forfeitures and other penalties which those unfortunate individuals incur who attempt unsuccessfully to evade the tax, it may frequently ruin them. . . . The law . . . first creates the temptation, and then punishes those who yield to it.

'Fourthly, by subjecting the people to the frequent visits and odious examination of the tax gatherers, it may expose them to much unnecessary trouble'.

We will, with your permission, consider these observations in the light of recent events. Mr Callaghan last April decreed that the Selective Employment Tax should produce a total of £315 million in the fiscal year ending 5 April next.

That was the estimated net yield. The reimbursements and premiums to the lucky employers were shown in the Civil Estimates to require £312 million in the current fiscal year, making a grand total of £627 million.

There will be 31 weeks of collection before 5 April 1967, and the gross weekly yield of the tax should therefore be over £20 million. In fact, however, in the first three weeks, the gross receipts have averaged £9 million a week.

What's gone wrong? Well, I know a bank which was worried about keeping within the 105 per cent limit on its advances. It asked its branch managers to check up with customers to see that they could pay their SET without asking the bank for more money.

One branch manager interviewed a farming customer. The farmer said he had no intention of buying any of those so-and-so stamps until twenty-four hours before the reimbursement next year.

This, of course, is highly illegal. That being so, I cannot condone the farmer's attitude. But, by golly, I can understand it. When the tax was first announced the academics cooed with delight over the cunningness of it. One point which particularly pleased them was that employers, even those who got refunds or premiums, would be making a forced loan, interest free, to the Government for four months.

Farmers and other chaps close to nature, with something like 400,000 employees, could on this argument be lending Big Jim nearly £14 million without return. There comes a point where the worm turns. By universal consent, this is a stupid tax. It will cost £100,000 to take the money from the farmers and then to pay it back to them.

Our farmer chum thinks this is a load of nonsense and refuses to subscribe to it – in more than one sense of the phrase. The chances of the Government catching up on him are nil. Only if an employee leaves need the card be stamped up to date.

One thing is certain. Our farmer friend is not alone. The initial yield of the tax proves that – although, as many big employers buy their stamps monthly, this will improve. But other strange things are happening. Part-time workers all over the country are suddenly working only 7½ hours a week instead of eight, and the boss doesn't pay SET. All sorts of people are suddenly becoming self-employed, and they don't pay it either.

In the end, of course, Big Jim will get his money from the farmer and other people who put off buying the stamps. But the early deflationary impact of the tax looks like being a lot less than it was expected to be. Indeed, prices will have been raised in August and September to meet a tax which often won't be paid till December, which is an odd concept of deflation.

But the main point is that SET has opened the door to one of the biggest tax fiddles in our tax history. This isn't surprising. If people think a tax is just and sensible they may not like it but they will pay it. If they think it's unjust, or stupid, or vindictive, they'll find ways of dodging the column. And when the thing develops on a major scale, the Government just can't win.

Come to-morrow, I report with sorrow, you are likely to see another pretty big tax fiddle. Dealings then start in the new ICI loan. On this, the Pink 'Un last week said thus: 'A huge turnover in the stock seems certain, with sales of small lots being readily absorbed by institutions who want to make up their requirements'.

How many of the stags are going to remember to include the £2 10s or £5 premium, or whatever it is they get, with their income for the fiscal year ending 5 April 1967, as a short-term capital gain? What possible hope has the already hopelessly overburdened Inland Revenue of checking up on those who don't?

Moreover, this isn't the end of the story of the capital gains tax. Because it has removed the inner circle of wealthy speculators which used to supplement the dwindling resources of the jobbing mechanism, there has been one of the sharpest falls in Stock Exchange values in recent memory. Turnover has shrunk to almost nothing. A firm of brokers was hammered last week.

This combination of circumstances must have had some influence on industrialists' attitude towards the investment the Prime Minister is so anxious to see industry making. It must have caused a major reduction in the yield of stamp duty and the income-tax and surtax the Stock Exchange community pays. It has proved singularly ineffective in influencing either the attitude of the militant left or in producing worthwhile redistribution of wealth.

It has caused a great waste of expert manpower; the trustee department of one bank, having spent years streamlining the department to reduce its staff, overnight had to increase it again by 10 per cent. In the light of all this, re-read, if you will, Adam Smith's four maxims.

## Tariffs and Taxes

Years ago I debated with one of the leading lights of the Labour Party, on steam radio, the merits and demerits of a capital gains tax. I asked him whether it would apply to houses or farms, and if it did, did he realise that the householder in an inflationary age would have to move from a four-bedroom house to one with three, and the farmer from a 300-acre farm to one of 250 acres, if they chose to sell. I asked why, if houses were exempted, as they would have to be as too many votes were involved, the man who put £5,000 in shares and lived in a flat should be penalised compared with a man who put his £5,000 in a house.

As we came out of the studio, the Labour chap – who is one of the nicest men imaginable – took my arm and said: 'Harold, you know I know absolutely nothing about a capital gains tax'.

And that just about sums it all up. Some eighteen months ago I got into fearful trouble because I suggested Mr Callaghan should send he-who-mustn't-be-mentioned back to Cambridge, the idea being that he could delight everyone there with his immense virtuosity and do the minimum amount of harm.

But perhaps some benefit will come out of it all. When we were trying to get into the Common Market, I attended many conferences on the harmonisation of our taxes and tax system with those of the Six. Sooner or later, you could always rely on at least one character getting up and saying that it wouldn't be a case of harmonising taxes and tax systems. The real problem would be to harmonise tax morals.

We have indeed until quite recent times been an astonishingly moral people where taxation is concerned. But if the Treasury and you-know-who produce many more Finance Acts like those of 1965 and 1966, we shall be able to enter the Common Market on equal terms in at least one respect.

# 6

# Everyday Economics

# Two voices are there

31 May 1960

THE mind of any columnist with frequent and regular deadlines to meet becomes, inevitably, something of a stockpot. Into the pot you throw ideas, thoughts, phrases, quotations – and you leave them there to stew. They go on stewing while you're mowing the lawn or falling asleep or having your hair cut, and when the need arises you fish the idea, thought, phrase or quotation out of the stockpot, done to a turn (you hope), and hey presto, there's your article.

A week or so ago into *my* stockpot went the idea of describing and discussing the two economic archetypes of this day and age. You know them, of course. You must do, regardless of the country in which you live. On my right, the type which used to be known as 'liberal' (small, non-political 'l'). Believes that even in the twentieth century we can still learn something from Adam Smith. Believes that the market place can decide most things better than the gent in Whitehall. Prefers bank rate to special deposits. Prefers, in fact, freedom to direction. On the whole, pretty inarticulate and not very good at stating his case. Probably the present day equivalent of the type Keynes had in mind when he talked in the *New Statesman* of the 'elder parrots'.

On my left, 'the moderns'. Dashing, dogmatic: or alternatively, with larger than life chips on their shoulders: the economic John Osbornes. Impatient and intolerant of orthodoxy, The Establishment, and of course, mumbo jumbo. Dirigistes to a man. Believe inflation to be not only inevitable but rather delightful. Very fluent, very vocal. Very good on the telly, where they reduce the Elder Parrots to speechless rage.

Well, there the idea was, in the stockpot, on the hob, simmering away nicely. I would, I thought, develop the rather intriguing thought that whenever their country starts to run into trouble, the liberal, freedom-loving school wants restraints imposed, whereas the dirigistes say 'To hell with it, let things rip, let the pound (or the dollar or whatever currency may be involved) go to pot. Production's the thing; investment's what matters. Vive le laissez-faire'.

I thought I might reflect on the fact that if this country would only make up its mind which basic philosophy of the two it wanted to follow it would certainly do better than it does by being so broad-minded about both that it doesn't know where it *is* going. The difficulty about this, I would point out, is that the choice would involve acknowledging that both have their imperfections. That, for example, economic liberalism means harshness, and economic dirigisme loss of freedom. And that we have an infinite capacity for kidding ourselves that we can have the best of all worlds and will go on dodging the issue almost indefinitely.

Or I would discuss the dilemma of which the economic John Osbornes, from Harold Wilson downwards (or should it be upwards?) are always apparently blissfully unaware – the fact that the countries they hold up to the Elder Parrots, as furnishing a shining example to fuddy duddy places like Britain and the United States, happen to have got where they are by following policies of which the dirigistes not only strongly disapprove but regard as positively immoral.

And so on. And so on. You will I hope concede that considering that the idea hadn't been in the stockpot for more than a week it was stewing away to some purpose. Quite a good article there, I was beginning to think. And then what happens? There I was, minding my own business, sitting quietly in the garden enjoying the sun and reading my two favourite Sunday newspapers, and what do I find?

What do I find indeed but two eminent protagonists of both schools of thought holding forth in their own inimitable style. Well, of course, the temptation was irresistible. Maybe the idea ought to have stayed in the stockpot longer. Maybe it shouldn't. Maturity or topicality? I've been a journalist too long, I'm afraid, not to seize such a chance.

I read Alan Day first. In the *Observer*. I must say I thoroughly approved of his opening. 'It is a bad sign', he said, 'when the Chancellor has to exhort businessmen to sell more abroad. . . . If industry is not exporting enough, it is because the state of the economy fails to encourage sufficient exports. It is the Chancellor's own job to deal with that'.

George, I thought, would have approved of that. (I must confess I always read the *Observer* first.) George Schwartz, of course. And there he was, sure enough, writing away in the *Sunday Times*, pointing out that we could in the ultimate choose between allowing the price mechanism or rationing to sort our priorities for us. Said George:

'Price works without any nagging, exhortation or threats, which is more than can be said for Government control of the economy. Price

# The Business of Capitalism

doesn't adjure you to play the game, you cads; it doesn't lecture you on the balance of payments; it doesn't threaten an autumn Budget. It displays itself in the window and leaves things to your judgment. As a result, most people live within their incomes, which means that they don't take out of the system more than they put in'.

Has it got you worried, this unanimous condemnation of exhortation by Mr Day and Mr Schwartz? Has that fellow Wincott been writing his usual rubbish about the Two Voices? Steady the Buffs! It all comes right in the end. 'What is really disturbing', Mr Day goes on, 'is the longer-run implication of the fact that our payments position tends to become distressingly weak each time our economy is reasonably fully employed. We are, in fact, suffering from the "new gold standard" which was established when we returned to convertibility, in the same way as we suffered under the old gold standard in the late nineteen-twenties....

'The big question is whether it is really sensible to-day to play the rules of the gold standard game: namely, fixed exchange rates and a policy of deflation to deal with payments difficulties. Is it not time to accept that sterling and the dollar are both a little over-valued – perhaps by 10 per cent or so – with the result that our exports are not quite competitive enough?'

So there you are. It *had* to come right in the end. There really are two voices. May I add a third, an elderly parrot sort of voice? Will Mr Day answer a few questions? Are we suffering from the rules of the gold standard game, new or old, or are we suffering from an attempt, as an economy, to take more out of the system than we put in? Was it the rules of the gold standard game which forced us to devalue in 1949 when we were neither on the gold standard nor had a convertible currency? Precisely where is the evidence of a policy of deflation to-day? If recurring devaluations and rubber exchange rates are the sensible things to have, why did France get into such a mess in the forty years up to 1958 that she had to have a near dictatorship to stop the rot?

# Keynes up to date

## 12 March 1963

WE all know our stuff on Keynes these days. Lord Robbins sums it up for us in twenty-three words in the first of the collection of his papers published this week.* 'It is the duty of states, through their budget and through the control of money, to maintain an appropriate stability of aggregate demand'.

Even ordinary people like you and I can spell out the theory of the thing. When things are on the up and up, you should have budget surpluses, higher interest rates and higher taxes, and you should encourage economy and thrift. When you run into a depression, you should have budget deficits, cheap money and lower taxes, and you should encourage spending and lavishness.

Particularly to those of us who really knew what a depression was, it all made so much sense it wasn't true. And it wasn't. Philip Snowden went on producing his 'nasty Boodgets'. Neville Chamberlain took us from Bleak House to Great Expectations which didn't materialise. We talked about inflation and a Stock Exchange boom – and we regarded an annual average of a million-and-a-half people on the dole as a normal feature of a normal world.

All that, of course, is old hat, pre-war stuff. How are we doing now? We all know our Keynes these days. Ay, there's the rub. Keynes himself was nothing if not honest. Defending the Bretton Woods agreements in the House of Lords just before he died, he said:

'Instead of maintaining the principle that the internal value of a national currency should conform to a prescribed *de jure* value, it (the Bretton Woods plan) provides that its external value should be altered, if necessary, so as to conform to whatever *de facto* internal value results from domestic policies, which shall themselves be immune from criticism'.

Now whatever the rights and wrongs of what Keynes said in 1946, you can't expect people who own and use money – which is all of us – to ignore what they said, for the simple reason that events proved them right. So we all know our Keynes these days. I myself saw speculators in New York buying US Government bonds at the end of 1957, with the banks putting up 95 per cent of the money, knowing full well the

* *Politics and Economics*, Macmillan 25s net.

131

rules of the Keynesian game demanded lower interest rates and therefore higher bond prices at that stage of affairs. The wide boys were in and out in a matter of weeks, having doubled what money they did put up, and within six months the market in US Government bonds was a shambles.

The Canadian dollar wasn't devalued last year because of the force of opinion outside Canada. It was devalued because the Canadian Keynesians themselves willed the devaluation. Again, I myself heard them doing so – at least two full years before the event.

Sterling was under pressure last week, having been remarkably firm for a long while and having withstood the shock of the breakdown of the Brussels negotiations with much less damage than most people expected. We should not blame the foreigners for last week's weakness and for any further weakness which may ensue. We should put the blame where it belongs – here, at home.

Mr Nicholas Kaldor is known to be one of the team of economic experts which Mr James Callaghan, the shadow Chancellor of the Exchequer, regularly consults. We mustn't suppose, of course, that Mr Callaghan slavishly follows the advice this team gives him, although it is unfortunate that he should air taxation ideas with which Mr Kaldor has in the past been associated.

But when Mr Kaldor advocates devaluation of the pound in the correspondence columns of *The Times* as the way out of difficulties which may arise from expansionary policies, we should not be surprised if foreigners decide they would rather hold other currencies. Equally, when the National Institute of Economic Research, which is financed in part by British industry and whose officers include many notable public figures, parades the same argument, we mustn't blame 'the gnomes of Zurich' if they start getting nervous.

Nor is it only abroad that you see these signs that we are all Keynesians now. In September, 1957, when we had a 7 per cent Bank Rate for the first time in the post-war period, 2½ per cent Consols were yielding 5.5 per cent. In July, 1961, when we had a 7 per cent Bank Rate for the second time, 2½ per cent Consols were yielding 6.4 per cent. At the beginning of 1959, which was broadly comparable with the present stage of the reflationary cycle, 2½ per cent Consols were yielding 4.7 per cent; to-day, the return is 6 per cent.

These are clear indications of a flight from money. You'll find confirmation of that flight elsewhere. British equities to-day are dearer, in terms of earnings yields, than equities in the Common Market or in the US. British equities to-day are not absolutely higher than they ever have been, but they are certainly dearer than they ever have been, at least since records of earnings yields have been available, so that you can argue they are *relatively* higher than they have ever been.

To-day, the earnings yield on the old FT Industrial share index is 7.16 per cent. At the comparable point in the reflationary cycle of 1958–60, it was around 12 per cent. Even at the all-time peak of the share price index in May 1961, the earnings yield was 8.61 per cent. If things go on as they have been going on for the last six years, it is not altogether outrageous to suggest that we may one of these days have a reverse yield gap between the yield on Consols and the earnings yield on equities. It would be nice to think that the present earnings yield reflects a general belief that we are facing an era of unparalleled prosperity. One suspects, however, that the real reason is that here again the implications of the Keynesian approach in modern conditions are sinking in.

The irony of all this is, of course, that the more the owners of money and money stocks become aware of the fact that they are the lemon in the Keynesian scheme of things, the more difficult and dangerous does it become to use that scheme. Clearly, we ought to have lower interest rates now. But already at the shorter end of the market any further rise in bank advances is going to force Mr Maudling to choose between a rise in rates or buying the banks' bonds himself. Is he also to do a Dalton in the long-dated and irre-deemable stocks, at a time of 'courageous spending', to force rates down? He could have to buy an awful lot of stock.

We are, I think, a slow-moving race. Looking back over the post-war period, it is almost incredible how long it has taken the owners of money to wake up to what has been going on. Even to-day, as I was pointing out last week, our investment mentality is utterly different from that of investors on the Continent. Yet because of the enormous weight of monetary debt in Britain – a weight untouched by currency purges, little reduced (in Continental terms) by the relatively slight inflation we have had, constantly added to by profligate governments – we are terribly vulnerable to any flight from money and money stocks.

Yet slowly but perceptibly, under the inexorable pressures exerted by our politicians, we are becoming a nation of wide boys. Did I not read a letter in the Press somewhere recently arguing what a good thing it would be under Mr Callaghan's wealth tax to mortgage one's house in perpetuity? Wider still and wider.

# Labour policies: the influence of Cripps

16 June 1964

JOKING apart, it is fascinating to try to foresee the financial and economic policies which a Labour Government is likely to impose – if the country decides it wants the Socialists next October.

The central figure must, of course, be Harold Wilson. This is not to say that the other leaders of the party will not play their part; the Labour Party is certainly stronger in economists than the Tories. But it's probably fair comment to say that Harold Wilson will not need a Chancellor of the Exchequer so much as an efficient tax collector.

I have had the impression for years that Mr Wilson's economic thinking has been powerfully influenced by that great person the late Sir Stafford Cripps.

This is natural enough. Simultaneously with Cripps' appointment as Minister for Economic Affairs at the end of September, 1947, Wilson, then only 31, succeeded Cripps as President of the Board of Trade and held that post until 1951. When Hugh Dalton resigned as Chancellor in November, 1947, Cripps succeeded him, and his dominance as economic overlord – and hence his influence on Wilson – was thereby increased, not diminished. It is worth while to look back at what happened then.

Great man though Cripps was, he was the complete planner. If you're too young to remember those days, you'll think I'm making this up. I can only say it's gospel truth. The British economy then really was 'a creature that moves in determinate grooves, in fact not a bus but a tram'. At least, that was the idea.

The Economic Surveys laid down each year in the most meticulous detail exactly what was going to happen. Of course, not all the controls and planning in the most regimented economy in the free world could keep the tram on the tramlines, but that didn't deter the planners.

The most incredible episode happened in September, 1947, when Cripps produced a schedule of export targets. The makers of needles, who had exported needles worth £80,000 in the last quarter of 1946, were given a target of '£0.085 million' for mid-1948 – and let off lightly with the same target for the end of 1948. Makers of lawn-mowers were told to get a figure of £55,000 up to £100,000 and £140,000 respectively by the middle and end of 1948. For brooms and brushes, the figures were £170,000, £250,000 and £300,000.

Planning with a fine toothcomb? It was indeed – even though the comb-makers were given targets (£100,000) identical with what they had achieved in 1946.

Harold Wilson is too sensible to try to repeat this nonsense, particularly without the controls of which he used to boast he had made such a splendid bonfire. But when you recall the atmosphere in which his formative years as a Minister were spent, you begin to understand his overweening confidence to-day that he knows exactly what industries and imports are essential or tolerable, and which should be penalised or replaced.

There's a precedent even for the 'ruthless discrimination' he now talks about. Way back in 1947, Cripps laid it down that if the needle-makers of Britain didn't reach their export target, there'd be no needles diverted to the home market; indeed, the needle-makers were to have their materials and labour withdrawn as a punishment. To the best of my knowledge, braces and belts weren't in the list. If they had been, we might all have gone round in 1948 holding our trousers up.

That was one side of Cripps. There were others – and it was in these others that the real greatness of the man emerged. The burdens he assumed were tremendous, and to the public, of course, he became the apostle of austerity. And indeed he was austere in his fiscal policies. His budgets were tough and lost his party votes, notably in the local elections of 1949. He followed the time-honoured policy of taking side-swipes at 'the capitalist' in an attempt to buy trade union support for the forerunner of an incomes policy.

Yet he could tell the TUC annual conference that if company profits were cut by a quarter it would only mean 4*d* in the pound to wages and salaries. He could tell the trade unionists how necessary it was to remove 'all those old-fashioned rules and regulations that can hamper a higher efficiency'.

You can find echoes of much of this in the Wilson of 1964. The belief in detailed planning ruthlessly applied and the anti-capitalist stuff can be taken for granted. On interest rates, he has said that while he will if necessary use short-term rates to safeguard our reserves, financial policy will have as one of its objects 'a general lowering of interest rates'.

There are those who believe this will mean a return to Daltonian tactics. I doubt this. Cripps in his first Budget reduced expenditure from the £3,181 million Dalton had envisaged in the autumn of 1947 to £2,976 million, and increased the surplus from £270 million to no less than £790 million. The national debt at 31 March 1949, was £25,168 million compared with £25,612 million two years earlier.

If Wilson really wants lower interest rates, he doesn't need to look beyond what happened in the gilt-edged market under Selwyn Lloyd and the present Chancellor to reinforce the experience of the Crippsian era. (Then, despite the collapse of the Daltonian campaign, the yield on 2½ per cent Consols ranged between 2.96 and 3.65 per cent!) And, indeed, at Swansea, Wilson said: 'The Budget must harmonise and not conflict with the Cabinet's decision about the rate of expansion. . . . It will have to provide in the Budget surplus for some of the capital needed for new investment'.

And yet. And yet. Would Cripps have said, as Wilson did: 'The key to a strong pound lies not in Britain's finances but in the nation's industry?' Would he not have made – did he not in fact make – the two co-equal? Did he not put a limit to food subsidies, and tax what are known as working-class commodities more heavily?

And here we approach what is likely to be the Labour Party's Achilles heel. There is no room for dispute now between the parties about the fact that total public expenditure can only increase whoever wins the election. Apart from a normal increase in borrowing, there will be the extra burden for the gilt-edged market inherent in Labour's nationalisation policies. Labour's spokesmen criticised the last Budget, and said they would have taxed the very industry on which Mr Wilson says we depend rather than the consumer.

In other directions, too, Labour is pledged to the artificial stimulation of consumption. Already, for example, there is uneasiness in the party over the impression that has grown up that Wilson has contradicted what other spokesmen have said about subsidising local authority housing through a differential interest rate. This isn't surprising, for a very substantial reduction of the 'interest burden' on council housing is the very stuff of local Socialist politics.

To all this, and a great deal more, Labour has two stock answers. First, that they will be able to get more out of an already fully employed economy than the Tories have done. Secondly, that higher taxation of capital and industry will cover both increased expenditure and provide the Budget surplus of which Mr Wilson talks, while allowing more scope for the consumer.

Both are acts of faith. On the first, Labour can expect to benefit temporarily from the honeymoon period the TUC will grant it in its early months. But on the second, with nearly 70 per cent of all net personal incomes concentrated in the hands of those earning £1,000 a year and under, and almost 95 per cent in the hands of those earning up to £2,000 a year, Wilson, like Cripps before him, will find that this is where the bulk of his budget surpluses must come from.

# Sir Winston Churchill and economics
26 January 1965

Sir Winston Churchill, it is said, had no interest in economic affairs. He was also often charged with the responsibility for Britain's return to the gold standard in 1925 at the pre-1914 parity and its consequences. Harold Wincott discusses these aspects of the great man's life.

How often do we read that Sir Winston Churchill was in fact a 'grass-roots economist'. I have the best of reasons for knowing this. In April, 1950, the late Lord Bracken told me that Churchill was to speak in the House on Stafford Cripps' Budget proposals. Would I present myself at Chartwell the next Saturday morning to offer what comments I could on Sir Winston's speech.

## The Business of Capitalism

It was an unforgettable experience. We went through the outlines of the speech together. We had lunch. Churchill disappeared for one of his famous cat-naps. I thought this was the cue for me to leave. But I was told very firmly that I must wait. I did. We resumed our discussions, and I left.

On the Monday morning came another summons – to 28, Hyde Park Gate. I have never seen such turmoil. The speech was being typed section by section, and brought in by a stream of secretaries. The sections were alphabetised, but 'M' followed 'A', and 'F' followed 'M'. Churchill, however, found nothing confusing in this, and gradually the whole thing took coherent and telling shape. At last the speech was ready and he was off to the Commons where he feared no man.

He paused for a few minutes to discuss with his staff that night's dinner. Lady Churchill had been away and clearly this was to be a very special reunion. Then a small procession formed, and Churchill went out to do battle with Cripps and Gaitskell.

The speech itself? The simile of the cow, 'the great advantage in a dairy is to have cows with large udders because one gets more milk out of them than from the others' – this because Cripps had boasted that the number of people with net incomes of £5,000 or more had been reduced from 11,000 pre-war to 250.

The need, and the opportunity then presenting itself, 'of regaining the economies, flexibility and conveniences of a free market such as has been successfully established in so many European countries, some of which were defeated in the war or long occupied by hostile garrisons'.

A nation divided 'not so much in enmity as in opinion'. Again, 'how long can we afford to be dominated by this ideological conflict which, as it paralyses our national judgment and action, must be deeply detrimental to an island like ours, with its 50 millions, growing only half their food?

'There is planning on both sides, but the aim and emphasis are different. We plan for choices, they plan for rules, and in this lies one of the aspects of our melancholy domestic quarrel'.

No economist? Not in any academic sense. But an unequalled gift, as in everything else, of expressing fundamental economic truths in language which ordinary folk could understand.

One needs no memento of such an experience. But I have one.

*Everyday Economics*

Five small magnetised metal cubes, spelling TATES. (Labour, you will recall, at one time planned to nationalise the sugar industry.) Churchill produced them at Chartwell, took them out of their box, took the letter S and pushed it towards the first T in Tate to make STATE. Push as he would the T repelled the S.

'You see', he said, with the slurred sibilation which all the world knew, 'it won't have it; it simply won't have it'. And he put the cubes back in the box and gave them to me. I still have them.

Let us go back then to what historians have judged to be Sir Winston's most important decision in the economic field.

Sir Roy Harrod has recorded in his *Life of John Maynard Keynes* that Keynes wrote three articles for the *Evening Standard* which he later published in a pamphlet entitled *The Economic Consequences of Mr Churchill*.

'Once thought of', Sir Roy continues, 'such a title was irresistible, if one desired one's words to be read by as many as possible. It did not imply that Keynes felt that much personal blame should be attached to Mr Churchill. His (Keynes's) attack was directed in part against popular clamour, but first and foremost against the experts who had advised the Chancellor'.

Nevertheless, historians have disputed endlessly about this. Said John Galbraith in *The Great Crash*:

'There is no doubt that Churchill was more impressed by the grandeur of the traditional, or $4.86, pound than by the more subtle consequences of over valuation, which he is widely assumed not to have understood'.

Galbraith, indeed, argued that 'in 1925 began the long series of exchange crises which, like the lions in Trafalgar Square and the street walkers in Piccadilly, are now an established part of the British scene'.

They still are, as we know to our present cost. Yet, Keynes apart, it is difficult to avoid the conclusion that the critics of the decision under Churchill's chancellorship to return to gold in 1925 have either attributed blame unfairly, or have misjudged the whole climate of opinion at the time, or are misdirecting their criticism.

It is not simply that most economic observers believe that while Churchill made the official announcement of the return to gold on 28 April 1925, the real decision was Montagu Norman's.

Norman himself was not alone. In June, 1924, Philip Snowden, first Labour Chancellor of the Exchequer, reaffirmed that it was the Labour Government's intention to carry out the recommendations of the Cunliffe Committee, which included a return to gold.

Yet another committee, the Chamberlain Committee, was willing in September, 1924, to recommend a return to gold 'if the internal purchasing power of the pound was adjusted to its external parity by credit control'.

This was the climate of most economic thinking of those times. The results were, of course, disastrous. But it is not clear that even Keynes was right in arguing that 'Mr Churchill's policy of improving the exchange by 10 per cent was, sooner or later, a policy of reducing everyone's wages by 2s in the £'.

It is true that later in the 'twenties and early 'thirties we did attempt by deflation to 'put the value back into the pound'. We are still paying the price to-day. But the late Professor Sir Henry Clay has argued that Norman (and hence, Churchill) 'could not know *then* that our exporters' chief competitors would subsequently fix the value of *their* currency at a level which gave them a lasting advantage in competition'.

Again, Professor R. S. Sayers has found it difficult to accept the thesis that all our subsequent troubles arose 'in any appreciable degree from the over-valuation of sterling in 1925.

'If', Professor Sayers wrote in an essay, 'Churchill had accepted the 4.40 argument we should still have had chronic depression in certain export trades, we should still have had the world slump and the international liquidity crisis, we should still have had the miseries of the 'thirties. It was basically the American trade cycle, and not British monetary policy, that made life so wretched for us'.

In the world of economics, as in everything else, Winston Churchill has no reason to fear the judgment of history. More positively, we can rejoice that for all our faults we order things better to-day, simply because we have learnt the lessons of history which he, more than any other man in our time, made.

# 2¼ per cent, or spitting in the foreman's eye?

18 January 1966

I FEEL I must write, as objectively and unemotionally as I can, about what has become a dirty word in the British economic dictionary – unemployment. I suspect as I start that there is so much to say that I shan't get it all into one article; if so, you'll have to put up with a second.

One thing is sure; the subject is topical enough in the opening weeks of 1966. We're all arguing about the chances of a national incomes policy working or not working, and Mr Ray Gunter, Minister of Labour (and in my book a splendid man), has warned that the only alternative to an effective incomes policy is 'considerable unemployment'.

Ultimately, Mr Gunter may be right. If eventually we run out of international goodwill and credit, if our exports aren't sufficient to pay for our imports of food and raw materials (and our other out-goings), and if we have no other cards to play, we might reach the position Rhodesia is expected to reach in a month or two.

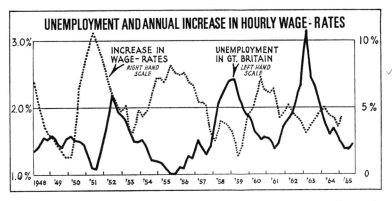

Yet I doubt whether many ordinary people took Mr Gunter's warning seriously. Why should they? For one thing, we aren't the only country which is faced with this problem. For another, in early 1962, Mr Selwyn Lloyd was saying time after time much the same thing as Mr Gunter is saying to-day. Within months, he was sacked from the Treasury and, subsequently, although we weren't within a bull's roar of an effective incomes policy, we were reflating to get rid of the unemployment which in 1962 averaged just over 2 per cent, and in 1963 (including one of the worst winters on record) 2.2 per cent.

Even if we do run out of international goodwill and credit, does it really follow that we should see massive unemployment? In 1949, one of Mr Gunter's colleagues in the present Government said: 'We devalued money because we refuse to devalue men'. Would Mr James Griffiths or any of his colleagues, faced with the same choice of courses again, choose differently?

Under the last Labour Government, as the saying went, we ate the Argentine railways for breakfast. Already Mr Callaghan has mobilised and partly liquefied the Government's holdings of dollar stocks. In preparation for what? Would these – and our other overseas assets – not go the same way as the Argentine railways if necessary to put off the evil day of large-scale unemployment?

No, the real problem is different. The real problem is one of persuading the British people that if they insist on carrying on as they have been carrying on we can't run our economy efficiently or even comfortably and decently so long as there is overfull employment. And on this you run slap up against the difficulty of defining what you mean by overfull employment.

I swear that if, after the experiences of the 'twenties and the 'thirties, Old Moore had guaranteed our people in 1945 that over the next 20 years they would never see the unemployment rate go over 3 per cent (except for a few weeks during a savage winter) no one would have believed him.

Of course, there have been extremes of views among Labour politicians. (The Tories don't seem to discuss the matter, at least not in public.) Sir Stafford Cripps was at least prepared to budget, in the Economic Survey of 1948, for an increase of 150,000 to 450,000 ($2\frac{1}{4}$ per cent of our working population then) in the numbers of unemployed, although in fact it never happened. Hugh Gaitskell accepted the definition of a 3 per cent average over good and bad years as constituting 'full employment'.

Mr Gaitskell, further, in an article in *Encounter* in November, 1955, accepted that there would be 'no need to worry about' a corrective process which involved an increase in unemployment from 1 per cent to 2 per cent, involving a rise of nearly 250,000 in the numbers of unemployed. (We were down to a 1 per cent rate, seasonally adjusted, at that time.)

On the other hand, of course, we had Aneurin Bevan's definition of full employment; quite simply, 'more jobs than there are men to fill them'. I'm not sure whether one other definition was Nye's but it might well have been: 'the state of affairs in which you can spit in the foreman's eye and get away with it'.

One may perhaps recall that Nye Bevan once described Hugh Gaitskell as a 'desiccated calculating machine', and that a certain young President of the Board of Trade resigned, along with Mr Bevan, in protest against Hugh Gaitskell's fiscal policies, when the latter was faced with the need for reducing an overwhelming volume of domestic demand in the spring of 1951. But young Presidents of the Board of Trade have been known to change when they get to 10, Downing Street.

In fact, as Professor Frank Paish has pointed out in his study 'The Limits of Incomes Policy', recently republished by the Institute of Economic Affairs, we discovered during the last war, when the services of every man and woman were desperately needed, and we were all conscripted and directed – and understood and accepted the need for all this – that the unemployment percentage never fell below about 0.7 per cent.

That happens to be about half to-day's level of unemployment. We also know that to-day about half of our unemployed people are only unemployed for two months or less, in other words are 'resting' as the actors say, or changing jobs.

A dynamic and changing economy – which is what we desperately need – certainly requires a bigger pool of mobile labour than this. But without it, it seems crystal clear that in fact a $1\frac{1}{2}$ per cent level of nominal unemployment in Britain – which is what we've had now for over a year – means no real unemployment at all in the accepted sense, but in fact a high degree of overfull employment.

The Paish Doctrine, as it has become known, is simply the proposition that whenever we attempt to run our economy with an insufficient margin of unused resources, including, alas but inevitably, human resources, we are unable to control incomes, particularly wage incomes, and run into balance of payments troubles.

Unfortunately, the evidence, of the past at least, to support Professor Paish, is overwhelming. Mr Paish does not rely on the unemployment figures alone. (This approach, as he acknowledges, is based on the work done by Professor A. W. Phillips and Messrs L. A. Dicks-Mireaux and J. C. R. Dow.) But he does argue that the minimum amount of unemployment which is feasible is 2¼ per cent as things are, or 2 per cent given a competitive labour market.

Looking for an earlier warning system than the relationship between unemployment and wage rates provides, Professor Paish has devised his own 'index of productive potential'. If the gross domestic product represents more than 95 per cent of the productive potential, says Mr Paish, look out for trouble. He expects it, not in 1966, when more elbow room may develop, but in 1968 or 1969, in a big way.

But the implications of a chart of the relationship between the changes in unemployment and wage rates, such as I reproduce to-day, simply cannot be gainsaid. (The rise in wage rates is measured from six months before to six months after the date shown, and is in consequence plotted six months behind that of unemployment. Who can doubt that when the wages figure for the third quarter of 1965 is plotted, to coincide with the low of unemployment about that time, it will act as it has always acted in the past?)

All this, of course, is historical. It may be that we can prove history to be the bunk Henry Ford said it was. That is something I shall discuss next week.

# On living with low unemployment

25 January 1966

W E didn't have to wait very long last week for a practical demonstration of the validity of the doctrine that if you run your economy without what Professor Paish regards as an adequate margin of unused resources you're bound to be in trouble. Questioned about the failure of the Coleshill gas plant in the Midlands, an official of the West Midlands Gas Board said quite simply: 'We had no reserve of plant available'.

Politicians, many of whom tend to be theoreticians, find it difficult to accept the Paish doctrine. Indeed, they fight elections in which they make lavish promises, and when challenged to say where the money will come from point to the unused resources, and calculate how many hundreds of millions their utilisation will add to the nation's wealth. Any industrialist will tell you how uneconomic are the last few percentage points of full capacity operation.

The vast majority of the great British public is also, understandably enough, opposed to the idea that the country as a whole would eventually be better off if we had another 250,000 unemployed. You can never be quite sure, can you, that you would not be one of the 250,000, facing a sharp drop in your standard of living, even if this proves to be temporary.

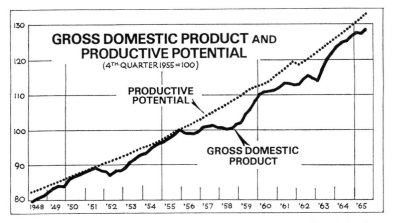

*Chart reproduced from "Policy for Incomes?" by F. W. Paish and Jossleyn Hennessy, published by the Institute of Economic Affairs (3rd edition).*

Because of this, the British are prepared to put up with the rather sordid, crummy society we now have. We get angry or worried about trains that are late, or cancelled, about the telephone booths that don't work, about the power cuts, about the increase in crime, about those jolly bank holiday week-ends on the beaches the young folk spend, with purple hearts in one pocket and contraceptives in another.

We get angry or worried about such things, we grumble about them, we throw out governments from time to time because of them, but on the whole we don't see them for what they are – the manifestations of a nominally over-fully employed economy. Not even when we hear that the casualty department of a hospital will have no doctor on duty after 7 p.m., because a doctor just isn't available. Not even when a child dies because the parents couldn't use a phone-booth, because thugs had smashed it up to get the cash, because there aren't enough policemen to keep an eye on the thugs.

This isn't entirely or exclusively a British phenomenon. When Professor Bill Phillips had done his researches into the relationship between unemployment and wages and prices in Britain over a century, two American economists did a similar exercise and came up with a similar conclusion.

Similar, but not identical. The critical level of unemployment in the States was found to be 5–6 per cent with an increase in productivity of $2\frac{1}{2}$ per cent. It will be lower now because the increase in productivity is higher. But have you noticed how in the last few months, as unemployment in America has fallen to about 4 per cent, the almost miraculous steadiness in prices there has come under increasing pressure? Have you noticed the language the correspondents in New York and Washington now use – about guide-lines, compulsory arbitration, and so on? It might be George Brown himself speaking.

If America's critical level of unemployment is high, reflecting the special social and economic and psychological conditions there, Western Germany's critical level is low, reflecting the special social and economic and psychological conditions there. Even so, as German unemployment has fallen below that critical level in recent months, so have the familiar troubles appeared to plague Germany.

In one infuriating respect, however, Britain's position is unique. It was all summed up in that programme 'Half-time Britain', produced, appropriately enough, by a half-time BBC. It is all recorded, again appropriately enough, day in, day out, week in, week out, by a half-time British newspaper industry.

It is the paradox that although, demonstrably, we are heading for trouble whenever the official unemployment level falls below, say, 2 per cent, we all know that if we ran this country as an efficient, modern country should be run, we should, temporarily and while we were sorting things out, have an unemployment rate running well into double figures.

Mr George Brown, and a good many of his colleagues (and I suspect a good many Conservatives too) believe first that we can make this a modern and efficient country without any rise in the present nominal level of unemployment, and secondly that we can do it by exhortation, or, if exhortation fails, as it is obviously failing, by legislation which, I read, will fine anyone who raises prices or wages or fees without getting Mr Aubrey Jones's say-so first.

On these propositions, I can only express my profound belief that if we insist simultaneously on upholding the first, the second just won't work, and even if it appeared to work the last thing it would produce would be a modern and efficient economy. It would instead in time produce an ossified, distorted and cheating society, and make our last state worse than the present.

On the first proposition, what we must do is so to reduce the level of demand in the economy, so to increase competitive pressures, that we do in fact create, temporarily, a sufficient margin of resources, including human resources, to sort things out, to enable us to get a level of productivity comparable with those of our competitors. And, of course, we must do everything possible to provide retraining facilities, adequate unemployment pay, and so on, while it is happening.

I have argued for a long time that the seeds of the mess we are now in were sown not by the Tories between 1951 and 1964, not by the Socialists between 1945 and 1951, but generations back: they were sown in the fact that we were the first major industrial power in the world; in the time, if you like, when we moved on from building wooden ships to ships made of iron.

It seems to me to be quite other-worldly to believe that the damage wrought by decades of industrial conservatism and protection, of living on the vast reserves our grandfathers and great-grandfathers built up, can be put right quickly, painlessly, or by attempts to preserve everybody's status quo.

And if you want to know how I think matters *can* be put right, not painlessly but quickly and surely, then I would say, as I have said in the past, there is only one answer, and that is by a phased reversal of the protectionist policy which we have followed to our cost for the last 35 years. If such a decision has to be accompanied by devaluation (which I don't, however, really believe must be the case) then I would accept that too.

The exasperating thing about it all is, of course, that simply because ours is a rather sordid, crummy set-up, there is no need to fear real unemployment in Britain for as far ahead as any of us can see. If we got our economic priorities right and, for example, we got our-

selves the sensible trade union structure that Germany has, and gave
our people the incentives to work the Germans have, and were as
willing (and able) to import as Germany is, there is no reason why we
too, in the long run, shouldn't run the country with a lower rate of
unemployment than we have done since 1945.

Of one thing I am sure. This should not be a matter of political
controversy between the two major parties here. The odds seem to be,
despite the showing of the January unemployment returns, that we
shall in fact see a rise towards a 2 per cent unemployment rate during
the current year. If that does happen, let us not have the Tories trying
to make political capital out of it. There will be plenty of scope (I
hope) for argument between Labour and Conservatives as to how
best to put right our fundamental troubles without trying to score
debating points over a trend which the Tories themselves engineered
more than once, and then lacked the wisdom or the courage to turn to
our permanent advantage.

# Use and abuse of economic freedom

21 June 1966

THE Labour Government, said Mr John Diamond, Chief
Secretary to the Treasury, at the recent conference organised
by the *Investors Chronicle*, wants an expanding economy ('more
resources') so that every individual can achieve economic freedom.

In the question period after his speech, Mr Diamond was asked to
explain what he meant by economic freedom. He gave these examples.
First, a man should have freedom to change his job when he wants to.
Secondly, he should be free to own another suit, apart from the one
he's wearing. Finally, he should not regard it as a complete tragedy (I
am paraphrasing) if he lost all the loose change in his pocket.

Gently, Mr Diamond pointed out to his audience, people in their
walks of life have always had these freedoms, and didn't know how
much they meant to the newly affluent. I think the audience took the
point.

I could add to Mr Diamond's definitions. I could, for example, point to the bright boys of the 'twenties and 'thirties who won scholarships for higher education and couldn't take them up because Dad was out of work, had been out of work for years, and the £1 a week the bright boy could then earn was a big item in the family budget.

In the circumstances of the 'twenties and 'thirties, as Mr Diamond implied but didn't say, political freedom was a fine theoretical concept but of very little practical value. The astonishing thing in retrospect is that most people accepted those circumstances as an Act of God in the face of which they were quite helpless.

They (and the politicians) know better now. It's indisputable these days that both political and economic freedoms are powerful forces. What are we doing with them? Certainly what Mr Diamond said we are doing. But other things as well.

On my recent visit to Western Germany I went by car. Between Bonn and Frankfurt I gave a lift to two lads, hitch-hiking, with the usual Union Jacks on their knapsacks.

One was on his way to Turkey, and expected to be away six months; previously, he worked for a men's store in London. The other, who used to work as a gardener for a local authority, was going to swing south-west from Mainz, down to Spain. He reckoned he would be away three months.

We talked quite a lot. They were decent kids. (I got a flat ten miles from Bingen, and they cheerfully changed a wheel for me.) They stayed at youth hostels. They made no attempt to learn any other language than English. Their main objective seemed to be to go as far as they could.

These kids had freedom to change their jobs when they wanted. They had spare clothes in their knapsacks. It wasn't a complete tragedy if they lost their loose change. (They worked a bit, illicitly, on the way. The chap who was going to Turkey had been to Spain last year, where he sold a pint of his blood for £3 10s. 'You can live for a long time in Spain on seventy bob', he said.)

I know a vicar in an inner London suburb. Among his flock is a chap who can't earn his economic freedom even in our present state of hyper-full employment. So he draws national assistance as well as unemployment pay. A few weeks ago, after drawing it, he called in at a betting shop and lost the entire £11 he'd just drawn.

He has a wife and five children, who had literally nothing to eat in the two rooms for which they paid an exorbitant rent. The wife came to see the vicar's wife, in desperation and tears. She left with a parcel of groceries.

Suppose the man had been given groceries rather than money by the authorities. Or that his wife collected vouchers for the groceries. Can you rule out the possibility that the husband would have flogged them and then lost the proceeds at the betting shop?

Three units out of a working population of 25,607,000. Not much to go on? Of course not. But it does happen, as Rex Winsbury pointed out in the May issue of *Management To-day*, that British industry loses nearly 100 times as many days a year through 'normal' absenteeism – as distinct from absenting yourself for six months – as it does through strikes, and that the annual bill is £220 million. (I doubt whether these figures embrace Ascot, Lord's and Wimbledon.)

Mr Winsbury argues very convincingly that good management can (and does sometimes but not often) do a great deal to cut down 'malingering'. And we should not assume that all 25,607,000 of us abuse our modern economic freedom spending the summer months mooching round Europe, or losing all our national assistance in a betting shop, or going sick when in fact we're hale and hearty. Indeed, ICI's statistics show that half its workers are almost never absent and that 16 per cent of them are responsible for 75 per cent of the absenteeism from which it suffers.

But the point surely is that in doing away with the conditions of the 'twenties and the 'thirties, in substituting the hyper-full employment of the 'sixties for the chronic unemployment of the 'thirties, in conferring economic freedom of the present order on everyone, we have placed too great a strain on human nature.

Mr Winsbury argues that the absenteeism he is discussing is essentially a management problem. This is as great an over-simplification as the other argument one is always hearing that the British working people (of all classes) are a bone-idle, lazy lot of good for nothings.

Given to-day's conditions; given the fact that the two lads I met in Germany have never known anything but overful employment and so believe that employers will be falling over themselves to re-engage them when they come back; given that the 16 per cent of ICI workers who account for three-quarters of the absenteeism believe equally firmly that if ICI won't employ them someone else will, it means that all your managers must be supermen. Well, perhaps that's an exaggeration. Let's settle for the proposition that they must all be above average – which my mathematical friends tell me is impossible.

Neither, of course, is it just a question of the loss of working hours. We are pitifully short of savings in Britain to-day. This isn't because we are a thriftless as well as a shiftless lot. Some mugs go on saving come hell and high water. But if everyone is so well cared for that an unemployable man is given £11 and provided with a betting shop in which to lose it on the way home, you mustn't be surprised if other people become sure that the rainy day will never come and so never provide against it.

My two boys now presumably sunning themselves in Turkey and Spain will doubtless expect a State pension, and one linked to the cost of living to protect them against inflation at that, when they reach the pensionable age. But what contribution are they making towards the real assets and the productivity, which alone can provide that pension, by opting out of Britain for up to six of each twelve months? Are they not in truth ensuring inflation everlasting?

In fact, is it not certain, in the long run, when economic freedom becomes so absolute, becomes in fact not freedom but licence, that no government, whatever its political colour, will be able to preserve that freedom, however highly (and rightly) Mr Diamond prizes it?

# Pros and cons of a free pound

2 August 1966

ODDLY enough, it was Mr Maudling's speech in last week's economic debate which, by general consensus, was the most effective. I say 'oddly enough' because in that speech Mr Maudling committed heresy. He actually discussed a floating exchange rate.

It was all right, of course. Mr Maudling supported the Government's decision not to devalue. He said bluntly that a floating exchange rate was no substitute for deflation. He admitted it was a difficult operation for a reserve currency such as ours, and impossible to contemplate when sterling is weak. But there it was. The words were said, and everyone agreed that it was a very constructive contribution to the debate.

The idea is not, of course, new. Eminent politicians-cum-industrialists like Lord Chandos and eminent economists like Professor Meade have supported it in the past. Even humble journalists like yours truly have said what Mr Maudling said last Wednesday – 'devaluation to a new fixed parity would be entirely wrong, and I am certain it could produce no good results'.

I have more than once in these articles stressed our peculiar aptitude – notably in 1925 and 1949 – in picking the wrong rates, the one too high and the other too low, and I have argued that a country's currency is like ICI's equity. It's just not realistic to pretend that its value is the same, decade after decade.

Now that Mr Maudling's speech – and the general reaction to it – have made the subject intellectually respectable again, my thoughts go back to a remarkable Hobart Paper* which was published at the beginning of this year. It was written under the pen-name of 'Spartacus', for the good and sufficient reason that the author is an economist in Government service.

It was a forthright attack on 'the "slavery" of fashionable ideas in economic policy', and it has not been made less relevant by last week's happenings. 'Spartacus' wrote of our advance towards autarchy, 'which will further tighten the protective bonds that hold Britain back from an advance to more competitive efficiency and strengthen the basis for a regimented economy'. These words are now seen to have had a truly prophetic ring.

His remedies were fourfold. In the reverse order in which he stated them they are the phased abolition of all import duties and quantitative import restrictions; the elimination of excess pressure of demand; the abolition of the fear of unemployment by strengthening the basis of personal security for people affected by competition; and the freeing of the pound.

The programme, you will appreciate, is not all that revolutionary. We have gone a good way towards meeting the demand that the fear of unemployment should be abolished. The Labour Party has stood on its head over excess demand and the unemployment that must result from its removal. Who knows but that one of these days the other two planks in 'Spartacus's' programme will not be adopted?

*Growth Through Competition*, Institute of Economic Affairs, 7s 6d.

*Everyday Economics*

It is the floating exchange rate idea that I want to discuss to-day. I suppose there are three principal arguments against it. The first is that it removes the pressure a fixed rate imposes on the politicians to follow 'sound policies'. That cock really won't fight in the light of our post-war history, will it?

Secondly, if a free rate meant a falling pound – as at times it would – we should, it would be claimed, be diddling our creditors. Here again, we have consistently diddled them, given a fixed rate, since the war-incurred sterling balances came into existence. But 'Spartacus' wants this criticism met by the transfer of the role of international banker from Britain and the US to an international agency which could then be provided with the necessary resources to support an assurance of a stable exchange value for reserves entrusted to it. This, you must admit, isn't a very likely starter at the moment.

The third objection 'Spartacus' doesn't mention. It is the possible worry and uncertainty that a floating rate for the £ might cause for the business world. Well, life hasn't been exactly a bed of roses for financial directors in these post-war years of fixity, and it *is* possible to cover forward risks in currencies.

Against these and other possible disadvantages, 'Spartacus' in fact pinpoints as the one overwhelming advantage of a floating rate that it would 'abolish the possibility of a balance of payments crisis'. This may sound a bit steep to you, but the argument behind it is sound enough, provided you remember the other planks of 'Spartacus's' programme, particularly the cutting of tariffs and the elimination of excess internal demand.

For 'Spartacus' in effect argues that the world's trading nations do not keep in step like a battalion of the Grenadier Guards. When we are expanding 'other countries are not necessarily engaged at the same time in a precisely similar upward movement of their economy and therefore their prices are not rising at the same rate. . . . A long-term discrepancy between Britain's price trend and that of other countries, which is a symptom of lack of competitiveness is a different matter; a temporary 'bottleneck' price rise (as the economy is preparing for expansion) need have no such long-term significance'.

Indeed, it is because the repercussions of an expansionary phase, such as the one Mr Maudling launched late in 1963 fall directly on the reserves rather than on the exchange rate that we get all the talk of 'national bankruptcy' at precisely the time when we are building up

153

the nation's potential. And because 'national bankruptcy' is so widely advertised, speculative pressure on the £, with the guaranteed limit to the speculators' losses provided by a fixed rate, automatically builds up.

We can, of course, regard all this as a purely academic discussion. Mr Wilson has staked his reputation on the defence of the existing parity and, with Mr Maudling, we can agree with the Prime Minister's stand.

But two things need to be said in concluding the discussion. There has been a pronounced secular tendency, demonstrated in my chart, for our crises to get worse as the years go by. And, of course, as this has happened, the remedies, within the context of a fixed exchange rate, get more desperate.

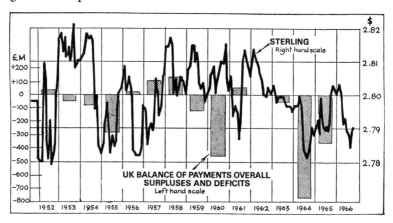

Moreover, as we were seeing last week, the orthodox package of remedies seems to become less and less effective. The Selwyn Lloyd package did put the balance of payments right fairly speedily, but even given the unemployment it created it didn't stop wages racing ahead of production or prices from rising. It may be the Callaghan package partially succeeded on balance of payments account – there is some evidence that the improvement 'did itself' – but it failed by all the other yardsticks. The patient seems to be developing an immunity to the old cures, and the onlookers overseas a corresponding scepticism.

This presumably is the justification for all the unpleasantness of last week. But however much Mr Brown may protest to the contrary, there is an authoritarianism in the latest Government measures which is very reminiscent of de Gaulle's authoritarianism in 1958, but, of course, without the devaluation of the franc and the discipline of the Common Market which went with de Gaulle's assumption of power.

I don't know whether Mr Brown had had the time to read 'Spartacus's' booklet. If not, he should do so. Not just for points I have been discussing in this article. But also for a reference on page 60 to what happened in Holland when employers were rendered liable to imprisonment if they paid more than officially approved wage rates.

If the bosses in what is surely one of the most disciplined and law-abiding countries in the world got up to the tricks 'Spartacus' describes, are we really to kid ourselves that in the fullness of time the same thing won't happen here?

If the choice is between last week's Bill and 'hidden inducements and dodges such as free lifts to and from work or gifts for employees (guitars, bicycles, etc.) and black-market operators making fortunes by hiring out workers at "black" wage rates', and a fluctuating exchange rate, I know which I would choose.

# Joining the private sector co-operative

## 28 December 1966

BEFORE Christmas, I was spelling out some of the practical – and serious – consequences which would follow if Parliament in its un-wisdom really did what a number of its supporters, including my friend Mr R. F. Fletcher, a director of the London Co-operative Society, are urging it to do – which is to turn every British company into a co-operative by paying off existing shareholders with a fixed interest stock, and ceding the equity to the workers in the businesses.

I dealt in that first article with the very serious repercussions such a move could have on the invisible items in our balance of payments, both outgoing and incoming; and also with the difficulties and anomalies of treatment of the new owners of the equity in British industry which would result.

# The Business of Capitalism

To-day, I want to discuss other very serious economic, fiscal and social consequences which Mr Fletcher's ideas would bring about.

First, some broad effects on savings and taxation. In general, to transfer the equity to workers would be to take it out of savers' hands and put it into spenders' hands. ICI has found that a distressingly high proportion of the shares it issues to its workpeople each year are flogged on the market as soon as they are issued.

Brother Fletcher, we can be sure, wouldn't allow this to happen, but a far higher proportion of the income on the workers' shares would certainly be spent than the proportion existing shareholders spend. Moreover, the yield from taxation of that income would fall sharply under the new dispensation. True, the high taxpayers would still pay heavy taxation on their fixed income 'compensation' stock.

But as time passed, and as Mr Callaghan's thousand years of prosperity (*anglice*, inflation) which he uses to justify the wrong-headed decision to adopt the £-cent-half system of decimilisation got under way, the yield from tax on 'unearned' income must meet a smaller and smaller part in the country's expenditure.

If that is true – and as Mr Kaldor's 1955 estimates of the long-term yield of capital gains tax were vitiated, as they would inevitably be under the new dispensation, and as the yield of death duties fell (as they would), the level of taxation on the beneficiaries of Mr Fletcher's scheme must increase, robbing them of some at least of the immediate benefits.

They would lose more of the benefits in other ways. The Socialists would have us believe that the equity of British industry is owned by the rich. Well, of course, wealthy people do traditionally own Ordinary shares, and the lower income groups traditionally invest in monetary media, which is one bad reason why the distribution of real wealth in Britain hasn't changed very radically during our lifetime.

But Mr Fletcher ought to realise that the company and the local authority pension fund, the insurance company, the investment and the unit trusts, the Church Commissioners, the charities, the trade unions, the university colleges and so on, are to-day owners of British equities on a scale that wasn't true 20 years ago. And all of them are investing in the main on behalf of people who are certainly not wealthy.

They haven't increased their holding of equities just for the fun of it. Their life would have been much simpler if they had stuck to the fixed interest issues which, by choice or by law, they previously relied upon. They changed their policy simply because in an age of inflation they couldn't meet their obligations without investing in real values – or as near to real values as they can get in this day and age.

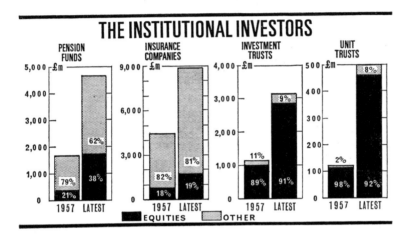

If Mr Fletcher converts each and every one of them into rentiers, that may give him a lot of personal satisfaction. But it will not get rid of the obligations now borne by these institutions. And since Socialists care for people (I am not being sarcastic, although I object strongly to the arrogant assumption that Socialists have a monopoly in this regard), the Socialists would have to take care of all the people whose financial position would be seriously damaged as the years went by and inflation (or prosperity) increased.

With a top rate of income taxation as high as ours is to-day, Mr Fletcher would therefore be faced with the choice either of abandoning his claim that he cares for people, or, again, of increasing the taxation borne by the lower income groups (to pay for the assumption by the State of these obligations) to an extent which would probably take care of any net benefits his scheme originally furnished them. Alternatively the cost of assuming the obligations (increased pensions) would whittle away the value of the 'workers' equity'.

Two things puzzle me about Mr Fletcher and people like him.

First, how people so intelligent can have failed to think through the vast, revolutionary and damaging repercussions of the deceptively simple proposition they propound. As we saw before the holiday, we are not just dealing with Mr Fletcher. The same idea has been put forward by men of the calibre of Jim Callaghan, Roy Jenkins, Austen Albu and Tony Crosland, and others I could name.

Secondly, I am forced to wonder what sort of a world they live in. The real world to-day is the world of the mixed economy, which happens to be a world in which, while the public sector does much admirable work, it is the private sector which, almost exclusively, does our export business and is the source of most of our revenue from taxation.

Some capable, sincere men who work in the same movement, or who have the same sympathies as Mr Fletcher, have accepted the facts of life in modern Britain. The Co-operative Insurance Society, for example, has over the last 11 years increased the balance-sheet amount it has invested in Ordinary shares from £19.9 million to £91.2 million, and the proportion that equities bear to total Stock Exchange investments has risen from 19½ per cent to 39 per cent.

It has done so because, in the words of Mr A. E. F. Lovick, J.P., the chairman, at the last annual meeting, 'our portfolio of Ordinary shares has enabled our policy holders to benefit from the increase in distributed profits which occurred during 1965'.

Indeed, if Mr Fletcher wants a case-study of what his scheme would do to pension funds, let him look at the record of the Co-operative Wholesale Society's pension fund. This fund has no investment policy. Employers' and employees' contributions are simply passed over to the CWS Bank. Originally, for many years the bank paid an annual interest rate of 4 per cent on the fund.

The fund did show a surplus in 1948, but latterly there have been consistent deficits which have been covered by supplementary grants by the CWS. Even including these grants, the return on the fund year by year has been sensibly lower than could have been obtained had the CWS pension scheme done what the CIS pension scheme did quite some time ago and withdrawn the funds from the bank and invested them independently on broadly the same lines that the CIS insurance funds are invested.

Although there was one modest increase a few years back, the average pension per CWS pensioner has, I believe, in recent years been about half the average paid by the pension funds of one of our largest industrial companies. All efforts by employees to bring the fund into line with more orthodox pension funds have been unavailing.

Now you may think I have blown this subject up out of all proportion. You may say that the speeches and writings of men who are now members of the Government from which I quoted last week were made a long while ago, and that these chaps have grown up since.

Maybe you'd be right if you did. Recently, Government spokesmen have got round to acknowledging that profits are essential. I think I have detected a note of embarrassment in the pronouncements of top Ministers when their backbenchers have been harrying them over company dividends.

But let's not beat about the bush. A lot of people in the world of business don't think these chaps have changed. And these are the people on whom we must rely if we are ever to become a high-investment, modern, efficient competitive economy able to support twice the population this country was built to support. Unless the Government wins the confidence of these people, we shan't do it.

If it is true, as I have said, that we are, all of us, in the last resort dependent upon the private sector, then let the Government declare openly that whatever reforms it believes are essential in that sector – and, Heaven knows, reforms are needed – it will have nothing to do with the doctrinaire, ideological nonsense that Mr Fletcher talks but will allow that private sector to flourish, making the best profits and paying the best wages and dividends it can.

And let Mr Fletcher realise that that so-called private sector is essentially a co-operative effort compared with which his movement is peanuts. (Although as Co-operator No. 5812, I have no wish to denigrate his movement.) If he wants to join the private-sector co-operative (as the CIS, the trade unions and many Labour-controlled council pension funds have done) I'll be pleased to recommend a good firm of stockbrokers or my favourite unit trust to him.

# 7

# The Smack of Firm Government?

# The light that failed

5 February 1963

AVID Low's historic cartoon of June, 1940, was of course an over-simplification, as all great cartoons must be. We were not alone, even in the darkest days of 1940. We had the active help of the Commonwealth, the token but psychologically vital representation of the occupied countries in our midst, the brightening skies in the West. So it is to-day, in an economic sense. We are alone, and yet not alone.

Yet with all the significant moral support we have discovered in the outside world in the last week, there can be no doubt that we must in the main work out our own economic salvation in 1963 and 1964, just as in the main we worked out our own military salvation in 1940 and 1941.

This is the moment of truth; the days of gimmickry and self-delusion must end. Every thinking person knows, deep down, has known for years, that there are many things fundamentally wrong with the British economy. These things are not to be cured by palliatives such as devaluation, import controls, reflation, a doubling of the price of gold, resort to the IMF, raising or lowering of Bank Rate. These palliatives merely buy us time to ensure that the fundamental troubles, the ossification of much of our economic structure, continue and worsen. Unless and until we put these things right, David Low's Britisher in 1963 will have his hands tied behind his back and an old man of the sea clinging to his shoulders as he tackles his task.

I tell you frankly that where our politicians, and particularly our Conservative politicians, are concerned, I have become so cynical it isn't true. Ever since 1951 I have heard them pounding tables, getting red in the face, proclaiming passionately that these fundamental troubles must and would be put right, not just temporarily, but once and for all. Six months, 12 months later, all the resolution had gone out of them. If I sound bitter in this article, remember that.

They're at it again, now. 'We must be ready', said Mr Macmillan in his television broadcast last week, 'to get rid of obsolete ideas'. 'Ready'? After over 11 years of Conservative government?

'We must ourselves do more to stimulate competition in British industry', said Mr Maudling in Oldham. Who does Mr Maudling think he's fooling? That remark of his was reported on column 2 of the front page of *The Financial Times* on Saturday. On column 7, 'Lex' had this to say about the take-over of Whitehead Iron and Steel by Mr Maudling's creature, Richard Thomas and Baldwins: –

'The terms are far above any "investment" price and RTB is unlikely to let Whitehead "shop around" for cut-price billets again'.

Does that sound like stimulating competition? Oh yes, I know Mr Maudling went on to say that 'while we must retain, and possibly even strengthen our protection against monopoly, we must also be prepared to look at consolidation within industry'.

So we must. But on the record, if there is to be a benefit in the shape of capacity production of steel billets to compensate for the reduction in the number of suppliers, is that benefit likely to be greater with the nationalised RTB as the supplier than it would have been with the free enterprise Stewarts and Lloyds?

On the record. It so happens that before the breakdown of the Common Market negotiations I was busily ferreting around for information concerning our nationalised electricity generating and supply industry to see whether the charges which have been so freely made that that industry has 'failed the nation' during the recent bitter weather were justified or not. The results of my ferreting are, I submit, highly significant, not only in that context, but in the far wider context of the fundamental problems which face this country now that we have got to put right of our own volition the maladjustments our membership of EEC would have forced us to tackle.

In the main, for comparisons of our experience in electricity I turned to that other lame duck of the West, that other country the slick young economists reckon to be dragging its feet in the various league tables of economic progress – the United States. The results set out here are in part attributable to the work done by Mr Robert A. Gilbert, an American who is president of the Intercontinental Research and Analysis Company, in *Barron's Weekly* and elsewhere, but my own researches, and consultation with experts here, satisfy me that what follows is in fact as accurate as such international comparisons can be.

The private enterprise v. nationalisation issue is complicated because the United States itself has what the Americans call 'socialised electricity', which produces approximately 20 per cent of the total American output. What we can say, however, is that the privately

The Business of Capitalism

owned US electricity industry sells something like 600,000 million kWH of electricity a year, produced by 340,000 people, whereas it takes 200,000 people in England and Wales to sell 104,000 million kWH. In short, it takes one private enterprise employer in the US to sell 1,765,000 kWH each year; here, each nationalised employer sells only 520,000 kWH. In the ultimate, our nationalised labour force in electricity is less than a third as productive as America's private enterprise labour force. If we achieved their standards of productivity we should need not 200,000 workers in this industry but 60,000.

In part, this glaring discrepancy may reflect the advantage, albeit a diminishing one, the US has in its hydro-electric stations. But it also reflects our reluctance to build really large plants or to adopt high steam pressures, temperatures and voltages. But even as we have increased the size of our plants, so has our total labour force increased, whereas in America the use of larger plants has brought the labour force down.

That isn't the lot, by a long chalk. As we endanger people's lives in hospitals, or shiver, or have to stop work, it may or may not comfort you to know that America's private enterprise electricity industry has an excess capacity represented by a safety margin of over 30 per cent.

Or take the actual load factor. This is the average ratio to the peak load of all electricity produced during any given period; the higher the load factor, the greater the efficiency. Our load factor in 1961–62, at 49.0 per cent, was actually lower than it was in 1948–49. America's rose from 60.8 per cent in 1948 to 65.9 per cent in 1960.

As you contemplate your electricity bills you ought to remember that America's private enterprise industry pays much heavier taxes than our nationalised industry does, and has to service all the capital it raises and pay dividends to its shareholders. Despite the alleged financial advantages of nationalisation, the average price we pay per kWH has risen from 1.35 cents in 1948 when the State took over to 1.72 cents in 1960–61 and 1.80 cents in 1961–62, whereas the US figure has come down from 1.90 cents in 1948 to 1.82 cents in 1960. It wasn't always thus. Between 1926 and 1940, our prices fell 41 per cent, America's by 37 per cent.

This price trend presumably reflects two factors, apart from the operation of Parkinson's Law. First, our industry – the one, true growth industry we have – can't finance itself in the capital markets and in consequence has to soak the consumer to provide funds for new plant and depreciation for old at a rate which by US standards is excessive. Secondly, despite our one monopoly buyer, our capital costs for construction are way ahead of America's; we seem to be both terribly conservative and lavish in the construction of 'outdoor' plants.

Withal, consider this. The American industry is composed of a diversity of units, sprawling over a continent, controlled by a Federal Power Commission, often hampered by local state politics. Here we have a highly organised industry in a small, densely populated country. If ever nationalisation ought to be able to deliver the goods, it is surely in our electricity industry. Manifestly, it hasn't.

I've strayed a long way from my starting point, you're saying? I don't think so. This is part of the old man of the sea round British industry's shoulders as it stands alone, outside the Common Market.

# The case for a Conservative opposition

9 July 1963

THIS article starts from the now generally accepted premise that although the Profumo affair was the ultimate cause of the decline and possible fall of Mr Macmillan and the Conservative Government, the real causes are of much longer standing and are much more deeply rooted.

Granted that premise, however, there is still no general agreement as to what the real causes are. I would not suggest that the problem I discuss here is the only one. But I am sure that it transcends all the others in importance, and I am equally sure that until a solution to it is found no government of whatever party or under whatever leadership will achieve more than temporary success.

This problem is, I submit, simply that no branch of government – central, local authorities or nationalised industries – has yet come within a bull's roar of coping with the simple fact that since 1900 expenditure by the public sector as a proportion of the gross national product has risen from 14 to over 40 per cent; from £280 million a year to over £10,000 million a year.

This failure to adapt the machinery and management of the public sector to the needs of the second half of the twentieth century has I'm sure in large measure been the penultimate cause of Mr Macmillan's recent troubles. 'The little local difficulties' of 1958 were in fact neither little nor local. They were symptomatic of this basic problem. So was the night of the long knives of almost 12 months ago. Was it not the spectacle of apparently lavish pay awards to dockers and electricity workers and the niggardly rises proposed for nurses which was primarily behind the events of 13 July 1962?

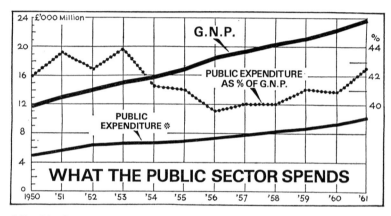

*Combined current and capital account expenditure of central and local governments plus capital account expenditure of public corporations.*

Mr Macmillan over the years of his leadership has built up a reputation for attempting to solve problems by sweeping them under the carpet, for appointing committees, courts, tribunals and so on to deal with awkwardnesses; and then, more often than not, failing to do anything about the recommendations of these bodies. I think this reputation is justly earned. But could not the explanation for this behaviour be that the whole machinery of government is still more suited to the days when men walked in front of horseless carriages with a red flag than to the days of jet aircraft, rocketry and nuclear energy?

You can get away with a gay wisecrack; with the pooh-poohing of the importance of an increase of a mere £50 million in public expenditure (when in the next four years such expenditure rises by over

## The Smack of Firm Government?

£2,300 million); with shelving your problems – while your luck lasts. But when your luck changes, these things are remembered and recoil on you. Faced with the hopeless task of running the modern State with quite inadequate machinery, you can either kill yourself in the attempt to cope with every niggling detail – as I suspect Anthony Eden nearly did – or you can delegate to the greatest possible extent – as I suspect, Mr Macmillan does. And then you delegate to the wrong man, and he goes to bed with a harlot.

Certainly I would argue that Sir William Haley would be spending his time more profitably in examining the social implications of this juggernaut of public expenditure which no modern government is able to control, instead of arguing that our troubles are the result of affluence or eleven years of Tory rule. Public expenditure at this level makes inflation absolutely inevitable. A public sector of this size inefficiently run is bound to give rise to the gross waste and extravagance which we all know goes on. Is it not in truth inflation, public waste and extravagance which have corrupted general standards in Britain in recent years, just as these things have corrupted other nations in the past?

Now if you accept this diagnosis, the logic of the situation forces you to some strange conclusions. It is, I think, quite hopeless to expect the Labour Party to tackle this question of expenditure and organisation of the public sector. For one thing, as I recently pointed out here, the Socialists believe passionately in the public sector – this is what Socialism is about.

The Labour Party is bending over backwards these days to appear to be the soul of sweetness and light. But already it stands committed to expanding the public sector in industry, in education, in local government, in housing, in pensions, in the social services and so on. Equally, the Socialists face two inherent difficulties in making the public sector more efficient. First, in office, once the initial honeymoon period is over, they will surely get bogged down in current detail and unable to sit back and consider the problem as it has to be considered, any more than the Tories have. Did not Stafford Cripps 15 years ago – when the calibre of the party was far higher than it is today – confess that a Labour Government stumbled from crisis to crisis and from expediency to expediency?

Secondly, the Socialists as egalitarians are likely to be more inhibited in modernising the public sector than the Tories would be.

167

# The Business of Capitalism

You'll remember, of course, the shocked surprise which Dr Beeching's £24,000 a year caused – and Dr Beeching certainly wasn't the highest paid director at ICI. I seem to remember the mutterings Alf Robens caused when he actually bought a plane the better to do his work at the Coal Board.

In local government, we have dedicated men running what are in fact very large businesses for salaries an executive in private industry would think pretty mean – but the Socialist councillors tend to fight any increase on principle. In central government, quite apart from the fundamental question whether we recruit the right type of person, so far from getting the influx of top people from industry the American administration secures, the traffic in the top ranks of our administration is all the other way. It is difficult for a Labour Government to tackle problems like these.

The Tories are much better equipped to do the job – but, in the nature of things, not in office. The younger element of the present government, under the tutelage of Rab Butler, did a remarkable job out of the public eye between 1945 and 1951. They not only changed the image of the Tory Party. They gave that party an impetus which, with the elbow room the post-Korean depression provided, impelled the Tories forward in the first half of the fifties with a success and a vigour they have not since experienced.

The Tories would be much less inhibited in tackling the problem of size of the public sector. Here, of course, it will never be the 'glad, confident morning' of 1900 again. We have not even yet, I think, accustomed ourselves as a nation to the idea that the public sector which was adequate with a 10 per cent unemployment rate cannot possibly cope with the highly prosperous private sector inherent in a 2 per cent unemployment rate; this is self-evident in roads, airports, schools, transport, housing, and so on.

Equally, however, scope must exist for reducing or limiting the public sector in other ways. The Tories in opposition could, for example, really examine the question of denationalising the gas and electricity industries, which could surely be done. They could examine the indiscriminate nature of so much of our social services which all too often perpetuates poverty and hands out unneeded largesse.

And, for obvious reasons, they are much better suited than the Socialists to tackle the whole question of modernising the organisation and methods of the expanded public sector which the conditions of the second half of the twentieth century are anyway going to demand. With all the criticism of Mr Macmillan and his government in recent years, they have done signal service to the nation in appointing (and giving a relatively free hand to) men such as Lord Robens and Dr Beeching.

I warned you that the logic of accepting my diagnosis – and frankly I don't think it can be rejected – would force us to some strange conclusions. It seems that whether Mr Macmillan stays or goes in 1963 or 1964 is irrelevant. It seems that the real, long-term interests of Britain would best be served in fact if the Tories lost the next election and, going into opposition, gave themselves the time to solve the outstanding problem of our age.

# How to lose the goodwill of business

18 May 1965

IT is one of the privileges of a financial journalist's job that it brings him to constant contact with the leaders of this country's industry, commerce and finance. It was because of what these people said to me last autumn that I knew the Labour Government had a very considerable volume of support among them.

They were, to be frank, browned off with the Conservatives who, after we failed to get into the Common Market – and for various other reasons – seemed to have lost all sense of direction. (It is worth recalling that even before these events a conference was held at Brighton in November, 1960, under the auspices of the FBI, in which for the first time one sensed that our industrial leaders were getting angry about Britain's performance; the support industry has given to the Department of Economic Affairs since last October reflects a continuation of that mood.)

The chaps I spoke to six months ago knew that democracy demands an effective alternative government; they would cite the price Canada paid for an overlong spell of one-party government; they thought Labour better equipped to deal with some of our problems than the Tories were; they hoped that the Labour Party of the 'sixties would have outlived the dogmas of the 'forties.

# The Business of Capitalism

I have to report to you from what I hear to-day that this goodwill is largely if not entirely exhausted. Why? For two main reasons, both bound up with Mr Callaghan's new taxes, although obviously the steel affair hasn't helped. The first concerns the manner in which the major reforms inherent in them are being rushed through. I listened last week to a team of leading tax experts bemoaning the fact that the opportunity for a really constructive reform of our fiscal system was being wasted; indeed, misused in such a way that grave damage must be done to this country's best interests.

It is all being done, of course, in the name of modernisation and speed. Where we had the Tory Mrs Mopps who swept the problems under the mat, we now have the Labour Mrs Mopps armed with a brand new and very powerful vacuum cleaner. The trouble is that the new charladies at the Treasury and the Inland Revenue haven't yet realised that, instead of sucking, the machine will blow the dirt and the grit all over the place. It's a sad thing to say, but the dirt and the grit did less harm under the rug.

It is all very reminiscent of the way in which Labour in 1945 found itself committed to a programme of nationalisation without, on the party's own admission, having any real idea of how to implement the programme. Labour talks of the Tories' thirteen wasted years between 1951 and 1964. But so far as tax reform is concerned, Labour itself wasted those years.

Only between January and June 1964 was it decided to adopt the Kaldor programme. Then the country had to be committed to the thing in Mr Wilson's first hundred days. Because of this, the country's best brains are spending and will for months ahead spend, most of their time trying to assimilate the enormous complexities of the Finance Bill instead of grappling with the real problems which face us.

The second reason why this Government has lost the goodwill of the world of business is because business now sees it as a government dominated by dogma. 'We used to ask ourselves what was the difference between the Tories and the Socialists', said one very distinguished man to me recently. 'And we thought there was none', he went on. 'We now know there is a difference. A Tory government uses taxes to raise revenue. A Labour government uses taxes to settle old scores; as a punishment.'

I am afraid this indictment stands confirmed in practically every clause in the Finance Bill. Because Labour is obsessed with the idea that a few wealthy individuals may run low-couponed gilt-edged stocks at a big discount against borrowed money, securing the eventual redemption profit tax free, it is proposing to immobilise the finest government bond market in the world, so that the market now discusses the possibility of eventual direction of institutional funds and a resort to tax-exempt bonds on the American pattern.

Because Labour has always been hostile to overseas investment, it is proposing to place serious handicaps of a permanent nature on some of our finest businesses. It conveniently overlooks the fact that the real strain on our balance of payments account over the last eight years has come from a doubling of government spending abroad and not from private investment, which has in fact remained static.

Here, of course, is more dogma. Public spending is sacred; private investment is expendable. What is being done about overseas investment is paralleled at home, where we have the application of a fierce credit squeeze on the private sector while public expenditure goes roaring ahead.

Moreover, the most naive arguments are employed to support the case against overseas investment. Mr George Brown writes to companies urging them to export more and invest less abroad, when in some cases not only have their past investments proved highly profitable and helped our exports of machinery and raw materials but it is literally physically impossible (or at least hopelessly uneconomic) for the companies to export their own products at all.

Again, presumably because Labour is obsessed with the idea that the well-off might benefit if the capital gains tax is imposed on the investor in unit trusts and not on the unit trust itself, the small investor in unit trusts is to be penalised because the trust will pay the tax at the higher company rate on any gains it realises whereas the small investor would be liable at a sensibly lower rate, and then only when he sells his units.

It is because of these and other manifestations that the Labour Party of 1965 is still in essence the Labour Party of 1945 that it has exhausted the very considerable goodwill it enjoyed six months ago. It is almost certain that none of this had much to do with last week's local election results; there, ironically enough, Labour lost ground in large measure because of the right things it has done.

But Mr Wilson would be foolish if he believed that his attempt to rush through a massive programme of ill-considered tax reform will not have its repercussions on the economy. Coupled with the credit squeeze, it must cause (in some directions is already causing) a considerable sense of frustration and uncertainty which will have its effects on investment plans and business decisions. Last November, Labour could claim with justification that the depression in the City was not shared elsewhere in the country. I doubt whether that is any longer true.

What really saddens me is this. Last October, before the election, I wrote an article here giving the reasons why, reluctantly I would vote Tory. I haven't the space to recapitulate them, although I'm bound to say that on re-reading that article practically every reason I gave has been justified by subsequent events.

The point is, however, that I concluded that article by saying that if there were reluctant Tories, there were also reluctant Socialists, although 'almost without exception you have to go a fair way down in the age groups to find them, and in the natural course of events it will take years before they can make their influence felt in the counsels of the party'.

Do we really have time to wait until these reluctant younger Socialists replace their older, doctrinaire colleagues, and give us the sort of radical but sensible alternative government reluctant conservatives have in, for example, the US? Or is it not our best hope that the swing to the Right evident last week will persist and bring the Tories back within the next six or nine months?

On the record, we should have to work pretty hard on the Tories to get them to do the things that have to be done. But on the record again, it could not be such a daunting job as that of modernising the party that believes it can modernise Britain by living to such a substantial extent in the past.

# Swizzles and squalid raffles

23 November 1965

'HALLO, Grandpa.'
'Hallo, Paul.'
'Having a snooze?'
'Well, I did drop off, Paul. Several big dinners in a row. Don't sleep as well after them as I used to.'

## The Smack of Firm Government?

'Grandma says it's the brandy.'

'Grandma's usually right, old man.'

'What happens at these dinners, Grandpa?'

'Well, you eat a lot and drink a lot and talk a lot. Then a gentleman in a red coat bangs a hammer and you drink the Queen's health and light a big, fat cigar.'

'The grandmas as well?'

'Not usually, Paul. Then a lot of important people at the top table make a lot of speeches.'

'Sounds awfully dull, Grandpa.'

'Depends on the speeches, Paul.'

'What do they talk about, Grandpa?'

'Depends, old man. On the chap. On the company. On the occasion. Last week I heard Mr John Diamond –'

'Who's he, Grandpa? Is he important?'

'I'll say. He's Chief Secretary to the Treasury. The Chancellor of the Exchequer's right hand man. A great benefactor to businessmen. Made their life simplicity itself by the two new taxes he helped to introduce this year. Standing in for the Chancellor, he was, on Wednesday night.'

'What did Mr Diamond say, Grandpa?'

'How important it was that we should all save a lot. Of course, it *was* the Actuaries dinner, and they're all concerned with savings. And how jolly well personal savings *were* going this year. Bit puzzled at that, I was.'

'Why, Grandpa?'

'Figures are funny things, Paul. I don't doubt Mr Diamond's were all right. But I'd been looking at some savings figures before the dinner. What we call National Savings. Very important. You know, National Savings Certificates, money in the Post Office, Premium Bonds –'

'Mummy says she's going to win £25,000 on her Premium Bonds, Grandpa.'

'That'll be the day, old chap. Anyway, on my figuring, National Savings are over £200 million worse off so far this year. And if you add in what we call Tax Reserve Certificates, we're over £250 million worse off. If the same sort of performance lasts until next April, we'll be over £420 million worse off. That's one reason why I was puzzled by the figures Mr Diamond quoted.'

173

'There's another, Grandpa?'

'Yes, Paul. A famous economist called Keynes worked out that if savings exceeded investment you got deflation, and that if investment exceeded savings you got inflation. I haven't noticed much deflation about, however well Mr Diamond says personal savings are going.'

'What's inflation, Grandpa? What you get after these dinners?'

'That's a different sort, Paul. The inflation Mr Diamond was talking about is, as he said, a wicked thing. He said it was dishonest to accept savings in one form of money and pay them back in another, worse form of money.'

'Don't understand, Grandpa.'

'One of these days. Paul, you may meet a very wise man called Old Squirt, and he'll tell you all about these things. Till then I'll do my best. Last week I was looking through my desk and I came across these.'

'What are they?'

'Post-War Credit Certificates. They represent savings I made over 20 years ago. Only the Government didn't trust me to make the savings myself. They made them for me. And they haven't trusted me with them ever since. But I shall be able to encash them very soon now.'

'You mean, you'll get your money back?'

'I wish I did, Paul.'

'H'm. Two of them. For over £126.'

'Mental arithmetic coming on, Paul.'

'Quite a nest-egg though, Grandpa.'

'It's a bit addled, Paul. It was £126 in 1942 and 1943 pounds. When the Government pays me my savings back, they'll be worth about £50 in 1966 pounds. I'll be able to buy less than a half of what I could have bought in 1942 and 1943. Put it another way. To make up for inflation, the Government should pay me £308, not £126. Of course, the Government got so conscience-stricken about the thing that they have been crediting interest – at 2½ per cent – on the £126 for the last few years. But I'll still only get 10s in every pound in what we call "real terms".'

'I say, what a swizzle, Grandpa. No wonder the National Savings figures are falling. And what a good thing Mr Diamond's going to stop it.'

'Paul, since Mr Diamond's been Chief Secretary, the pound's fallen in value nearly 5 per cent from 20s in October, 1964, to 19s in

## The Smack of Firm Government?

October, 1965. And the actuaries still say that money invested at 5 per cent compound interest doubles itself in 14 years.'

'H'm. I see what you mean about figures being funny things, Grandpa.'

'Depends on your sense of humour, Paul. At another dinner, on Thursday night, I heard Mr Fred Catherwood –'

'Who's he, Grandpa?'

'He's the Chief Industrial Adviser at the Department of Economic Affairs. Anyway, I heard Mr Catherwood tell the investment analysts that the Ministry of Labour's worked out an activity index which proves that the British people are the hardest workers in the world. Some of the people at that dinner thought *that* was pretty funny.'

*     *     *

'These National Savings, Grandpa.'

'Yes, Paul.'

'What can we do about them?'

'Well, one of the troubles this year has been that the building societies raised the interest rates they pay on savings left with *them*.'

'So people put money with the building societies instead of in National Savings?'

'Seems like it. Now the Post Office is going to increase the interest it pays –'

'And people will stop putting money in the building societies and stick it in the Post Office instead?'

'Maybe, Paul.'

'They want some new ideas, Grandpa.'

'Sir Miles Thomas would be delighted to hear from you, Paul. He runs the National Savings Movement.'

'Well, he's livened up the Premium Bonds, Grandpa.'

'He has indeed, Paul. I reckon he had an awful tussle with the Prime Minister to get the £25,000 prize idea through.'

'Why, Grandpa?'

'Well, when Mr Harold Macmillan introduced Premium Bonds in 1956 – he was Chancellor of the Exchequer then and the top prize was only £1,000 – Mr Wilson said in the House of Commons that a chap called Horatio Bottomley – he was a famous swizzler – was Mr Macmillan's inspiration. Mr Wilson called the Premium Bonds a

175

"squalid raffle", and said the Tories would be fighting the next election on the slogan "Honest Charlie Always Pays".'

'Grandpa?'

'Yes, Paul.'

'Suppose I wrote to Sir Miles and suggested the National Savings Movement ran bingo sessions.'

'In the Albert Hall. With Mr Diamond calling out the numbers. "Eyes down. All the fives, fifty-five. Clickety-click, sixty-six. Key of the door, twenty-one. Kelly's eye, number one. Never been kissed, sweet sixteen". I can hear the Chief Secretary doing it, Paul.'

'With the Prime Minister presiding.'

'And every now and then Mr Callaghan crying out "Honest Harold will shake the bag".'

'I'll write to Sir Miles right away, Grandpa.'

'Paul, if the Beatles got the MBE for their contribution to the national effort...'

# The devaluation of democracy

27 September 1966

WELL, the Liberal Party had a good romp at Brighton, didn't it? I'm not referring to the young bloods, bless them – although they clearly had a field day – but to the top echelon of the party. There was Lord Byers saying what we have all known for years – that because of over-manning, concealed unemployment and under-employment, so far from being short of labour, we have somewhere between 2½ and 5 million people available for productive work.

There was Mr Peter Bessell, MP for Bodmin, saying, on the very same day, that to Liberals 'one able-bodied man out of work is a crime; and we pledge ourselves not to rest until he is employed again'.

Now I don't know whether Maskelyne and Devant were Liberals. But I do know we're not going to shift Lord Byers' 2½–5 million under-employed folk into productive work by waving a magic wand and without committing a good many of Mr Bessell's crimes.

Of course, you can argue that the Liberals have a minimal chance of forming a Government, and that a minimal sense of responsibility is therefore all you can expect from them. But I must say I was shocked to read that Mr Heath, in his election-style tour last week, was seeking to make capital out of Mr Wilson's statement on 20 July about the future level of unemployment.

Mr Wilson, you may recall, said that, looking beyond our present troubles, beyond the reabsorption, the redeployment and the measures for regional distribution, if we had an unemployment percentage of between $1\frac{1}{2}$ and 2 per cent he did not believe such a figure would be unacceptable to the House of Commons. Mr Heath said Mr Wilson was 'content to see nearly half a million unemployed as a permanent feature of our national life', with the obvious implication that he, Mr Heath, wasn't.

I rate this statement by the Prime Minister as the most significant pronouncement any politician has made on our economic affairs since the war. It marks an end to make-believe. I've covered all this ground pretty thoroughly in the past, but I must restate the essential facts again.

There are three salient points. First, during the last war, with all its conscription into the services and industry alike and all its unique circumstances, the unemployment percentage never fell below 0.7 per cent. Secondly, half the unemployed in normal circumstances to-day find work within eight weeks; these are people who are 'resting' or moving from one job to another.

Finally, a Ministry of Labour survey found that in October, 1964, out of a total of 313,000 unemployed (about 1.4 per cent) 196,000 had been out of work for more than eight weeks; and of these 142,000 were for one reason or another virtually unemployable. The genuine national figures for unemployment then were 54,000 and the percentage rate about 0.2 per cent.

Now the academics debate among themselves the validity of the Phillips-Paish argument that, given an official level of unemployment below, say, $2\frac{1}{2}$ per cent it is impossible to control wages and prices; to keep increases in incomes within the bounds of the increases in the volume of goods and services on which they can be spent.

As an ordinary chap, I would have thought events over the last 20 years had proved Professors Phillips and Paish to be abundantly right. But since, for all our faults, it is not really excessive rises in wages (relative to our competitors) which have undone us, I am more concerned with other facts of so-called overfull employment.

# The Business of Capitalism

There are factories in this country – at least there were earlier this summer – which suffered a 100 per cent turnover in their labour force. This meant, to spell it out, that on 31 December everyone who was working there on the previous 1 January would have left. In practice, the position was even worse than that, because the managers and executives, and a certain proportion of the workpeople, were long-service people. So for 31 December, you should probably read 30 November or even 31 October.

Now whatever Mr Bessell and Mr Heath may say, these factories must, in the nature of things, have been operating way below maximum efficiency, and what goes for them goes in greater or lesser degree for the whole country. I talked about this to an American friend of mine, one of those strange admixtures America breeds – a Wall Street man but a great radical.

'Harold', he said, 'the management of such a factory wants its head examined. Give the workers a 5 per cent bonus provided they stay 12 months, a 10 per cent bonus at the end of two years, and so on. It would pay the company hands down.'

'And if the factory next door made it 10 per cent at the end of the first year and 20 per cent at the end of two years?' I asked. 'Would that really happen?' my friend replied. I told him it certainly would have in the conditions then prevailing, and he said, 'Well, I give up.'

So does management, and so long as this state of affairs prevails all the Departments of Economic Affairs, all the Prices and Incomes Boards, all the appeals to recapture the Dunkirk spirit will be of no lasting avail. An unemployment rate of just over 1 per cent places an intolerable strain on human nature.

Mr Wilson has had the courage to realise this. He has had the courage personally to take responsibility for measures aimed at reducing the level of demand and raising the level of unemployment. He is not the first politician in Britain to do so in the post-war years. But he is the first to tell the British people that when the present squeeze and all the readjustments which must follow it are over, they must get used to the idea of up to 500,000 people being out of work, and that they must give up the idea of work-sharing to frustrate the process.

Of course, other things must happen at the same time to alleviate hardship, to retrain people, to avoid unconscionable levels of unemployment in certain parts of the country. But the major basic decision has been taken. If Mr Heath seeks to make capital out of that decision. Mr Wilson will flay him alive – and on the Tory record, not without reason.

There will, in any case be plenty of other issues on which the Tories can criticise the Government. I believe Mr Callaghan had the truth in him when he told the Group of Ten five days after Mr Wilson's package in July that deflation and Government economies alone would do the job. But because, as the *New Statesman* has said, the crisis affords a wonderful opportunity to go ahead with full-blooded Socialism, we are lumbered, or probably shall be very shortly, with all the paraphernalia of socialist authoritarianism.

We've had it before, of course – only then a Labour Government inherited the controls – and in the long run it neither worked nor did the British people like it. History will repeat itself. The British are not naturally the nation of informers they are now being encouraged to become. Labour cannot take away from them the option of getting the hell out of it. Not just the doctors and the pilots and the footballers. But now I see even the bricklayers.

Labour will go on making mistakes, as it is already making mistakes. Chopping and changing its mind, for example, on the fiscal aspects of SET, whether it's to be passed on, or whether it's to hit profits and thus reduce investment. So overloading the Ministry of Labour with the mechanics of the same tax that the Ministry cannot now handle all the problems involved in the unemployment being created.

Let the Tories and the Liberals hammer the Government on issues such as these, but not on Mr Wilson's decision to end, once and for all, the state of impossibly overfull employment which has bedevilled the British economy for over 20 years.

Throughout the free world, it seems to me, democracy is being devalued by the politicians. As country after country allows demand to become excessive, employment overfull, so do the politicians funk tackling the problem at its roots – fiscal policy – and put altogether too much strain on monetary policy.

If Mr Wilson is the first to reverse the process, he will not just have made his place in economic history. He will have given this country the chance to show what it really can do, and that, I believe very sincerely, will surprise the world. We are not, begging Mr Gunter's pardon, an inherently dishonest and thriftless people. To the extent that we have become so, the politicians are to blame.